THE DURHAM NEW TESTAMENT GREEK COURSE
A Three Month Introduction

THE DURHAM NEW TESTAMENT GREEK COURSE

A Three Month Introduction

William G. Morrice

with a Foreword by

C. E. B. Cranfield

PATERNOSTER PRESS
Carlisle, UK

British Library Cataloguing in Publication Data

Morrice, William G.
  Durham New Testament Greek Course:Three Month Introduction
  I. Title
  487.4

  ISBN 0–85364–556–6

Typeset by Photoprint, Torquay, Devon
and printed in the UK by
The Guernsey Press Co. Ltd., Guernsey, Channel Islands
for the publishers

Contents

Foreword

I am honoured and delighted to be asked to commend Dr
Morrice's excellent *New Testament Greek Course*. I have read
it with very great admiration. It is the fruit of long experience
of instructing beginners in Greek by one who is a born teacher.
He is a most sympathetic and gentle guide – something which
all who are entrusted with the responsibility of initiating first
year theology students in Greek or Hebrew ought to be, but
which, unfortunately, not all of them are. Aware of the
pressures from which students suffer, some of whom have to
start learning two very different languages at the same time,
often nowadays without any acquaintance with Latin to help
them, he has been at great pains to explain everything as
clearly and as interestingly as possible. He knows that learning
Greek can actually be enjoyable and has striven to make it so.

I hope and believe that this book will be an effective
encouragement to the weaker students not to lose heart but to
persevere, as well as being a springboard by which the stronger
may be impelled to advance from strength to strength.

The importance of theology students' learning Greek cannot
be urged too emphatically. Having to depend on translations
can never be the same thing as reading the original. The person
who is without Greek is bound to be at a serious disadvantage
in studying the New Testament.

I wish all who use this course great joy in their studies. May
they have the good sense to persist in reading the Greek
Testament not just until their final examinations but throughout
their lives – to their own immediate benefit and to that of all
those whom they are called to serve.

C. E. B. Cranfield

Durham,
January 1993

About this Course

The aim of this course is to introduce students to Hellenistic Greek (also called Common Greek or the **KOINE**). Since the primary purpose is to enable students to read Mark's Gospel in Greek as soon as possible, most of the examples are taken from the first eight chapters of this gospel. The course was first produced for private circulation in 1991 in response to requests from First Year Honours students in the Department of Theology in 1990/1. During session 1991/2, it was used successfully in Durham and was also tried out by my brother at St Paul's United Theological College at Limuru, Kenya. I am grateful to those who have pointed out typing and other mistakes and have made suggestions for improvement—my brother, the Rev. Dr C. S. Morrice; Mr Bernard Robinson of Ushaw College, Durham; tutorial assistants in the Department of Theology: the Rev. P.R. Carrell, Mrs Elizabeth Fisher, Dr Peter Harland and Sister Rosemary Howorth; and several students. I also wish to express sincere thanks to Professor Charles Cranfield, who has not only written an over-generous foreword but also supplied me with a note of misprints and comments, some of which have been incorporated into this first printed edition; to Professor James Dunn, who entrusted to me the teaching of New Testament Greek to First Year Honours Theology students; and to my wife for her constant support and encouragement.

The plan of action in Durham over the past two academic sessions has been to ask students to study the first four chapters before they arrive. These are revised in four hours at the beginning of term leading up to a progress test. Thereafter, the class is divided into groups. Succeeding chapters are introduced in plenary sessions followed each week by two meetings in groups for consolidation, revision and completion of assignments. By the end of the first term of nine weeks, the complete course has been covered and students are ready to move on in their second term to the translation and exegesis of selected passages from the first eight chapters of Mark's Gospel in Greek.

The Greek New Testament recommended for use is that of the United Bible Societies edited by Aland, Black, Martini, Metzger and Wikgren. Students will find it convenient to have Barclay Newman's *Concise Greek-English Dictionary of the New Testament*, which can be obtained from the Bible Society bound along with the UBS Greek New Testament. The dictionary is referred to in this book as UBSD.

Finally, don't consider learning Greek to be a chore. It is well worth the effort you put into it. One cannot study the New Testament in any depth without some knowledge of New Testament Greek. In this case at least, the end justifies the means, but the means to the end can be enjoyable in themselves. Learning Greek can be fun. Make up your mind to enjoy it.

January, 1993   Wm G. Morrice

CHAPTER ONE

The Greek Alphabet

Alpha	α	A	Short as in "fat" or long as in "father"
Beta	β	B	Hard as in "big"
Gamma	γ	Γ	Hard as in "gong";
			-γγ- = -ng- as in "angle"
Delta	δ	Δ	Hard as in "dot"
Epsilon	ε	E	Short as in "best"
Zeta	ζ	Z	As in "zoo"
Eta	η	H	Long as the "a" in "mate"
Theta	θ	Θ	Short as in "thin"
Iota	ι	I	Short as in "fit" or long as in "feet"
			iota subscript – ᾳ ῃ ῳ – not pronounced
Kappa	κ	K	As in "kit"
Lambda	λ	Λ	As in "long"
Mu	μ	M	As in "mother"
Nu	ν	N	As in "not"
Xi	ξ	Ξ	As in "axe"
Omicron	o	O	Short as in "hot"
Pi	π	Π	As in "pit"
Rho	ϱ	P	As in "Rome"
			initial ϱ always has a rough breathing – ῥ or ʽP
Sigma	σ	Σ	As in "song"; ς at end of a word
Tau	τ	T	As in "Tom"
Upsilon	υ	Y	Short as in "duty" or long as in "moor"
Phi	φ	Φ	"Ph" as in "Pharaoh"
Chi	χ	X	"Ch" as in Scottish "loch"
Psi	ψ	Ψ	As in "lipsalve"
Omega	ω	Ω	Long as in "more"

§1   There are 24 letters in the Greek alphabet, many of which are similar to the corresponding letters in our own alphabet.

§2   The English word *alphabet* is derived from the first two letters of the Greek alphabet – ἄλφα . . . βῆτα.

§3   The first and last letters are found three times in the Book of Revelation.

Ἐγώ εἰμι τὸ ἄλφα καὶ τὸ ὦ, λέγει κύριος ὁ θεός . . .
Ego eimi to alpha kai to omega, legei kurios ho theos

ἡ ἀρχὴ καὶ τὸ τέλος . . . ὁ πρῶτος καὶ ὁ ἔσχατος . . .
he arche kai to telos . . . ho protos kai ho eschatos . . .
(Rev.1:8; 21:6; 22:13)

§4   As in English, there are both capital letters and small letters (or, lower case).

§5   The capitals are called uncials. It was in these uncials that the New Testament was originally written. The earliest complete manuscripts of the New Testament are uncial manuscripts. They are known as Codex Sinaiticus and Codex Vaticanus and originated in the middle of the fourth century.

§6   In the 9th century, the small letters came into general use. They are called cursives, since they could be written by running the hand along the line without lifting it from the paper – from the Latin **currere** = *to run*.

§7   Thus, later manuscripts of the New Testament are called "cursives" or "minuscules" (from Latin **minor** = *smaller*) as opposed to the "uncials".

§8   In our printed Greek texts, capital letters are used less frequently than they are in English. They are to be found at the beginning of proper names, of a paragraph and of direct speech, but not at the start of every sentence.

§9   English has five vowels – a, e, i, o, u. In Greek, there are seven vowels – α, ε, η, ι, ο, υ, ω.

§10   **Short Vowels**: ε and ο are always short, as in "best" and "hot".

§11 **Long Vowels:** η and ω are always long, as in "mate" and "more".

§12 **Short or Long Vowels:** α, ι and υ can be either short or long, as in "fat"/"father"; "fit"/"feet"; "duty"/"moor".

§13 **Diphthongs** (from φθόγγος = *sound*; and δίς = *twice*): These are sounds produced by two vowels sounded together – αι, ει, οι, αυ, ευ, ου and υι pronounced as **ai** (as in "aisle"), **ei** (as in "height"), **oi** (as in "oil"), **au** (as in "owl"), **eu** (as in "eulogy"), **ou** (as in "wood") and **wi** (as in "wick"). When a diphthong containing ἰῶτα is lengthened, the other letter is lengthened and the ἰῶτα is written underneath as **iota subscript** – thus, ᾳ, ῃ, ῳ. **Iota subscript** is not pronounced [see §18].

§14 **Gamma**, the third letter of the Greek alphabet, is used instead of **nu** before γ, κ, ξ and χ; e.g., ἄγγελος – **angelos** (= *messenger*); ἄγκυρα – **ankura** (= *anchor*); λάρυγξ – **larunx** (= *throat*) [see §24].

§15 **Delta** gives us the English word for *the mouth of a river* with its alluvial deposits, especially the River Nile, from its resemblance to the capital letter in the form of an equilateral triangle.

§16 There are several **double letters** in Greek – **zeta** (found in English as **z** as in "zoo"); **theta** (found in English as **th** as in "theatre"); **xi** made up of γσ or κσ or χσ (found in English in **x** as in "xenophobia"); **phi** (ph as in "pharmacy"); **chi** (ch as in Scottish "loch"); **psi** (as in "lipsalve").

§17 There is no letter **h** in Greek. Instead, every Greek word beginning with a vowel must have either **a rough breathing** to indicate an aspirate or "h" sound – ἁ . . ., ἑ . . ., ἡ . . ., ἱ . . ., ὁ . . ., ὑ . . ., ὡ . . .; or **a smooth breathing** to indicate its absence – ἀ . . ., ἐ . . ., ἠ . . ., ἰ . . ., ὀ . . ., ὐ . . ., ὠ . . . . These are placed over a small letter. They are placed to the left of a capital letter – ’Α . . ., ’Ε . . ., ’Η . . ., ’Ι . . ., ’Ο . . ., ’Υ . . ., ’Ω . . . . In the case of a diphthong, the breathing is placed above the second letter – e.g., αὐ . . . or οἱ . . . or Εὐ . . . .

§18 **Iota** is often written under the letters α, η and ω – ᾳ, ῃ and ῳ. This **iota subscript** can appear especially at the end of a word; e.g., in the dative singular of nouns and adjectives. However, it makes no difference to the pronunciation of the word and so it is an **eye diphthong** only, but it is very important to write it whenever it is required [see §13].

§19 **Nu movable** is found with certain endings to prevent a hiatus with a following word – i.e., a break between one word ending with a vowel and another word beginning with a vowel. In Hellenistic Greek, it came to be used even when there was no hiatus.

§20 **Pi** is very familiar in English especially as a mathematical symbol. It also comes into English in such words as *hippopotamus* (= *river-horse*). The Greek words are ἵππος and ποταμός. Can you guess which means *horse* and which means *river*?

§21 **Rho** is the equivalent of **r** in English, but when it occurs as the initial letter of a word it always has a rough breathing [see §17] – ῥ . . . or ῾Ρ . . . . This accounts for the peculiar English spelling of such words as *rhythm, rhetoric, haemorrhage*. Notice that the capital **Rho** is like English capital **P**.

§22 **Sigma** has two forms – σ within a word and ς only at the end of a word.

§23 **Tau** is the equivalent of t.

§24 **Upsilon** appears in English as y in such words as *sympathy* (συμπάθεια), *dynamite* (δύναμις = *power*), *gymnasium* (γυμνός = *naked*).

§25 There was little if any punctuation in early Greek manuscripts of the New Testament, but printed Greek texts use a fullstop and a comma as in English. A **question-mark** is written like our semi-colon – ; Thus, τίς; = *who*? τί; = *what*? There is a colon – a single dot at top of the line – ·.

§26 When a final vowel is omitted before a following vowel,

elision is marked with a single inverted comma or apostrophe
– ὑπ' αὐτοῦ (Mk 1:5).

§27 When a final vowel merges with a following initial vowel,
the smooth breathing remains to indicate **crasis**, i.e., *mixing* of
vowels (from κεράννυμι = *I mix*) – κἀκεῖ (Mk 1:35) from καί
and ἐκεῖ mixed together.

§28 There are three **accents** in Greek – acute ´; grave `; and
circumflex ˜. The acute can stand on one of the last three
syllables of a word, the circumflex only on one of the last two,
and the grave only on the last syllable. However, the new
student should not bother too much about accents, except in
a few cases [see §29].

§29 The accents give us little guide to pronunciation. Their
chief use in Hellenistic Greek is to distinguish between certain
words that differ only in accent; e.g., τίς; = *who?* and τις =
someone; τί; = *what? why?* and τι = *something*; εἰ = *if* and εἶ
= *you* (singular) *are* .

§30 There are no **quotation marks** in Greek. Instead, the
beginning of direct speech is indicated by a capital letter in the
printed text, sometimes with a preceding ὅτι (= *that*). This
ὅτι should not be translated except by quotation marks. See,
e.g., Mk 2:12 – . . . λέγοντας ὅτι Οὕτως οὐδέποτε εἴδομεν
= . . . *saying, "We never saw [it] thus"*.

ASSIGNMENTS

1. **PRACTISE** writing out the Greek letters, both capital and
small. **LEARN** alphabet by reading the letters aloud over and
over again.

2. Place a piece of paper over the Greek column below.
WRITE OUT in Greek letters the following English words,
which also happen to be Greek words, observing carefully the
long and short vowels and the breathings. Check your answers
by uncovering the Greek column.

Greek Words

anathema	ἀναθεμα
angel (-os)	ἀγγελος (= *messenger*)
basis	βασις (= *step*)
character (long final vowel)	χαρακτηρ
chorus (choros)	χορος
climax	κλιμαξ
cosmos	κοσμος
crisis	κρισις
diagnosis (long "o")	διαγνωσις
drama	δραμα
echo (both vowels long)	ἠχω
exodus (exodos)	ἐξοδος
genesis	γενεσις
hippopotamus (-os)	ἱπποποταμος
hypocrite (-es)	ὑποκριτης
Philadelphia	Φιλαδελφια
psyche (long final vowel)	ψυχη
rhythm (-os)	ῥυθμος
stigma	στιγμα
sympathy (-eia)	συμπαθεια
thesis	θεσις

3.   How many did you get right? Did you remember to insert smooth and rough breathings when required? Can you think of any other English words that are really Greek words or that are derived from Greek words?

4.   In learning Greek, it is important to practise reading it aloud and writing it out over and over again. It is essential to acquire a working vocabulary as soon as possible by reading and practice. **READ ALOUD** the Greek sentence in 1§3. **WRITE OUT** the Greek with an English translation – looking up the text in the RSV, if necessary.

5.   **LEARN** the following vocabulary. A useful method in the initial stages is to write the Greek word on one side of a card with the English translation on the other side. One can then test one's memory in both directions at odd moments of the day by playing cards with oneself!

ἐγώ	I	εἰμί	I am[1]
ὁ θεός	God	ὁ κύριος	the Lord
ἡ ἀρχή	the beginning	τὸ τέλος	the end

6. **NOTICE** the three forms of the definite article (= *the*) –

   ὁ (masculine)   ἡ (feminine)   τό (neuter)

The complete paradigm of the article will be learned in due course [3§7(1)].

7. Can you think of English words derived from the vocabulary you have learned so far? This is a useful aid to memorizing Greek words. The Greek word for *word* is λόγος [3§11]. It is found combined with other Greek words in many English words with the meaning of *study* . Consider the following English words and write down the Greek words from which they are derived. Cover up the Greek column until you have attempted to do the exercise on your own.

archaeology	ἀρχη and λογος
egotism	ἐγω
psychology	ψυχη and λογος
teleology	τελος and λογος
theology	θεος and λογος

8. What is the Greek word for *and* ? You should be able to work this out easily from 1§3.

9. **READ ALOUD** over and over again the Lord's Prayer (Mt.6:9–13).

---

[1] εἰμί on its own = *I am*. In 1§3, the personal pronoun is inserted for the sake of emphasis. For the present indicative active of the Greek verb *to be*, see 4A2 (Chapter 4 – Assignment 2).

CHAPTER TWO

The Greek Verb

§1 INFLECTIONS and PERSONAL ENDINGS in ENGLISH

(1)   In every language, each sentence or clause must have a verb or doing word. For example, Time *flies*. Salt *is* good. You *surprise* me[1]. In each of these cases, the verb is *italicized*. The subject of the verb can be a noun (time/salt) or a pronoun (you).

(2)   In English, the verbal form can vary slightly depending on whether the subject is a noun/3rd person pronoun or a 1st/ 2nd person pronoun and whether it is singular or plural. This is called **inflection.**

Person	Singular	Plural
1st	I speak	We speak
2nd	You speak (Thou speakest)	You speak
3rd	He/she/it speaks	They speak

(3)   The differences are more pronounced when the English verb is the verb "to be"

Person	Singular	Plural
1st	I am	We are
2nd	You are (Thou art)	You are
3rd	He/she/it is	They are

---

[1] These examples are taken from the Concise Oxford Dictionary, p.1369.

§2 INFLECTIONS in GREEK VERBS

(1) The Greek verb is much more highly inflected than the English verb. It changes even more from person to person and from singular to plural. To the basic stem, prefixes and suffixes are added in order to indicate the subject of the verb and the time or nature of the action.

(2) The **present indicative active** of λύω, which is used by grammarians as the model Greek verb, has a stem λυ to which endings are added to indicate person and number.

Person	Singular	Plural
1st	λυ – ω	λυ – ομεν
2nd	λυ – εις	λυ – ετε
3rd	λυ – ει	λυ – ουσι(ν)[2]

(3) One set of meanings of the present indicative active of λυω is:

Person	Singular	Plural
1st	I loose	We loose
2nd	You loose	You loose
3rd	He/she/it looses	They loose

(4) However, more often than not the Greek present tense expresses **continuous action** in the present − *I am loosing, you are loosing, he/she/it is loosing, we are loosing, you are loosing, they are loosing.*

(5) The Greek present tense can also express **emphatic action** − *I do loose, you do loose,* κτλ[3].

(6) Almost every Greek word has an **accent**[4]. As far as verbs

---

[2] Originally, this movable nu was inserted when the next word began with a vowel, in order to prevent hiatus. See 1§19.

[3] κτλ. stands for three Greek words καὶ τὰ λοιπά = *and the rest.* It is, therefore, the Greek equivalent for etc. from the Latin **et cetera**.

[4] See 1§§28f.

are concerned, the accent is usually recessive, i.e., it goes back in the word as far as it can. When the final syllable is short, one counts three back by inclusive counting and places an acute accent on that syllable. When the final syllable is long, one counts only two back. As already explained, students do not need to bother too much about accents. However, notice how the accents work for the present indicative active of λύω.

Person	Singular	Plural
1st	λύ – ω	λύ – ομεν
2nd	λύ – εις	λύ – ετε
3rd	λύ – ει	λύ – ουσι(ν)[5]

§3   VOICES[6]

(1)   The Greek verb has **three voices** , whereas English has only two – active and passive. The three voices in Greek are active, middle and passive. The active and the passive are used as in English.

(2)   A verb is in the **active voice** when its subject is acting or doing something (from Latin **agere** = *to act*); e.g., *he speaks.*

(3)   A verb is in the **passive** when its subject is spoken of as suffering (from Latin **pati, passus** = *suffer*) or as being acted upon or as being at the receiving end of an action; e.g., *he is being saved.*

(4)   In addition to the active and the passive, Greek has the **middle voice**. This is sometimes similar to the reflexive in French in that it may signify that the subject performs an action upon himself or for his own benefit. In form it is identical with the passive voice in four out of the six tenses; i.e., in the present, imperfect, perfect and pluperfect.

---

[5] For movable nu, see 1§19.

[6] See further Chapter 6.

§4   TENSES

(1)   In addition to having an extra voice, Greek has an extra tense. So there are six tenses – present, imperfect, future, perfect, pluperfect (all with rough English equivalents) and **aorist** .

(2)   As already explained in §2(3) – (5), the **present tense** in Greek is more often used to express continuous action in the present than to express a simple present, but it can also be used to express an emphatic action.

(3)   The Greek **future tense** can be translated by the English future tense: *I shall speak, you will speak, he/she/it will speak, we shall speak, you will speak, they will speak.*

(4)   The **imperfect tense** in Greek expresses continuous, habitual or repeated action in past time: *I was doing this, I used to do that* or *I kept on doing something else.*

(5)   The **perfect tense** can usually be rendered into English by the perfect tense with *have* or *has: I have written* or *God has spoken.* Its significance is that it represents an action in the past whose consequences remain in the present. Thus, *I have written* **[and it remains written]** or *God has spoken* **[and that is that!]** or **[and he must be obeyed].**

(6)   The **pluperfect tense** is translated into English by the pluperfect with *had : I had spoken, you had spoken,* κτλ.[7]

(7)   The important point about the Greek **aorist tense** is that it refers to a single action. Only when it is in the indicative mood does the aorist refer to past time – and then it is a single definite action; e.g., *I wrote* (once), as compared with the Greek perfect which refers to an action in the past whose consequences remain in the present – *I have written* (and it remains written and will not be changed).

(8)   Students should note carefully the difference between the **aorist tense** and the **perfect tense.** Compare the two statements:

[7] If you have forgotten the meaning of κτλ., see 2§2(5)n.

I closed the door [once in the past] – Greek aorist; and *I have closed the door* [and it is still closed] – Greek perfect[8]. See Mk 1:2 – γέγραπται = *it has been written [and remains written]*

§5 MOODS[9]

(1) There are six moods in Greek – indicative, imperative, infinitive, participle, subjunctive, and optative.

(2) As in English, the **indicative mood** is used to make a statement or indicate something or ask a question; e.g., *I am writing a letter. Are you sitting comfortably?*

(3) The **imperative** issues a command; e.g., *Learn this lesson! Be quiet!* In English, it sometimes takes an exclamation mark after it.

(4) The **infinitive** is expressed in English with "to" – e.g., λύειν = to loose.

(5) The **present participle** in English ends in "-ing" – thus, λύων = loosing.[10]

(6) The **past participle** in English ends commonly in -ed: e.g., *loosed* ; or in -en: e.g., *broken.*

(7) The **subjunctive mood** can usually be translated into English with may or might and is used, for example, in purpose

---

[8] For interesting examples of the perfect tense in the New Testament, see Jn 19:22 – ὃ γέγραφα, γέγραφα (though perhaps Pilate should have used an aorist followed by a perfect, but the aorist has been attracted into the perfect) = *what I wrote* [once in the past] *I have written* [and it remains written and I'm not going to change it]; Rom.8:38 – πέπεισμαι = I have been persuaded [and I am quite sure].

[9] See further Chapter 7.

[10] In the sentence, *Learning Greek is easy*, "learning" is a present participle used as a noun. However, in the sentence, *He is a man of great learning*, "learning" is an English noun meaning *knowledge.*

clauses – e.g., *I am doing this in order that you* **may** *learn Greek*;
or, *I did this in order that you* **might** *learn Greek*.

(8)　The **optative mood** (from Latin **optare** = to wish) is less frequent in Hellenistic Greek than it was in classical Greek. It usually expresses a wish. It can also express a doubtful or indefinite future[11].

§6　NEGATIVES

(1)　The **negative** with all moods except the indicative is μή, though οὐ/οὐκ/οὐχ is sometimes found with a participle, as in Mt.22:11; Lk.6:42; Jn 10:12; Acts 7:5.

διὰ τὸ μή ἔχειν βάθος γῆς (Mk 4:5) = *on account of not having depth of earth*

(2)　The **negative** with the **indicative mood** is οὐ (before a consonant); οὐκ (before a vowel or diphthong with a smooth breathing); οὐχ (before a vowel or diphthong with a rough breathing).

οὐ μέλει σοι; (Mk 4:38) = *Is it not of concern to you?*

οὐκ εἰμὶ ἱκανός (Mk 1:7) = *I am not worthy.*

ζητεῖτέ με οὐχ ὅτι εἴδετε σημεῖα (Jn 6:26) = *You are seeking me not because you saw signs . . .*

(3)　Both μή and οὐ/οὐκ/οὐχ can be found in compounds with other small words such as δέ (= *but, and*), ἔτι (= *still, yet*), εἷς, μία, ἕν (= *one*). Thus,

οὐδέ /μηδέ = *not even, nor*

οὐδέ . . . οὐδέ . . . / μηδέ . . . μηδέ . . . = *neither . . . nor . . .*

---

[11] See 7§8.

οὐκέτι / μηκέτι = *no longer*

οὐδείς, οὐδεμία, οὐδέν / μηδείς, μηδεμία, μηδέν =
no-one, nothing

οὔπω = *not yet* (Mk 8:21)

(4) In English, a second or double negative in a clause cancels the first one out.

I am not speaking to no-one = I am speaking to someone.
We cannot do nothing = We must do something.

(5) In Greek, double negatives do not cancel each other out. One can use two or even three in the same clause.

οὐδὲ ἁλύσει οὐκέτι οὐδεὶς ἐδύνατο αὐτὸν δῆσαι (Mk 5:3)
not even with a chain no longer no-one was able to bind him

καὶ οὐδενὶ οὐδὲν εἶπαν (Mk 16:8)
And to no-one nothing they said! **or** *They said nothing to nobody!*
or better *They said nothing to anyone.*

§7 CONJUGATIONS

(1) There are **two conjugations** of verbs in Greek, distinguished from each other by the ending of the first person singular of the present indicative active. The first has -ω, the second has -μι; e.g., λύω (*I loose*) and δίδωμι (*I give*).

(2) The **second conjugation** contains only a small class of verbs and is distinguished from the first conjugation mainly in the present, imperfect and aorist tenses. The second conjugation will be left till Chapter Eleven, though some – especially in compound form – are very frequent in the New Testament.

§8 FIRST CONJUGATION

(1) Most Greek verbs are in the **first conjugation** and follow

the pattern of λύω throughout all tenses, moods and voices. Even the so-called irregular verbs are inflected like λύω.

(2) Notice that the personal endings are added to the stem, which, in the case of λύω, is λυ-.

(3) In order to conjugate the present tense of any Greek verb of the first conjugation, take off the final -ω of the first person singular of the present indicative active (the form of the verb given in the dictionary) and add the personal endings.

Person	Singular	Plural
1st	λυ – ω	λυ – ομεν
2nd	λυ – εις	λυ – ετε
3rd	λυ – ει	λυ – ουσι(ν)[12]

(4) The 2nd person plural of the Greek verb must never be used when a single person is the subject. The 2nd person singular is always used in speaking of a single person while the 2nd person plural is kept for more than one person.

(5) The **future indicative active** is formed by taking the stem (λυ-), adding -σ- and then the same endings as for the present indicative active.

Person	Singular	Plural
1st	λύ – σ – ω	λύ – σ – ομεν
2nd	λύ – σ – εις	λύ – σ – ετε
3rd	λύ – σ – ει	λύ – σ – ουσι(ν)[12]

(6) All **past indicative tenses** have an **augment** preceding the stem. This takes the form of ἐ- when the stem begins with a consonant.

(7) The **imperfect tense** of λύω is:

Person	Singular	Plural
1st	ἔ – λυ – ον	ἐ – λύ – ομεν
2nd	ἔ – λυ – ες	ἐ – λύ – ετε
3rd	ἔ – λυ – ε(ν)[12]	ἔ – λυ – ον

[12] Notice the movable nu. See 1§19.

(8)   Notice that the 1st person singular and the 3rd person plural have identical forms. Normally, the context will show which it is.

(9)   When the stem begins with a vowel, **the augment** takes the form of lengthening - α > η; ε > η; o > ω. E.g., the imperfect of ἀκούω is ἤκουον.

(10)   The **aorist tense** is formed with the augment plus the stem plus σ plus aorist endings.

Person	Singular	Plural
1st	ἔ – λυ – σ – α	ἐ – λύ – σ – αμεν
2nd	ἔ – λυ – σ – ας	ἐ – λύ – σ – ατε
3rd	ἔ – λυ – σ – ε(ν)	ἔ – λυ – σ – αν

(11)   Again, notice the movable nu in the 3rd person singular.

(12)   The **perfect tense** has reduplication (the initial consonant of the stem plus ε) plus the stem plus κ plus perfect endings, which are identical with the aorist endings except for the 3rd person plural.

Person	Singular	Plural
1st	λέ – λυ – κ – α	λε – λύ – κ – αμεν
2nd	λέ – λυ – κ – ας	λε – λύ – κ – ατε
3rd	λέ – λυ – κ – ε(ν)	λε – λύ – κ – ασι(ν)

(13)   Notice the movable nu in the 3rd person singular and the 3rd person plural.

(14)   When the stem begins with a vowel, reduplication takes the form of lengthening of the vowel as for an augment. The perfect indicative active of ἀγγέλλω = *I announce* is ἤγγελκα = *I have announced*.

(15)   The **pluperfect tense** has the augment (though this is usually omitted in Hellenistic Greek), reduplication, the stem, κ plus pluperfect endings.

Person	Singular	Plural
1st	(ἐ)λε – λύ – κ – ειν	(ἐ)λε – λύ – κ-ειμεν
2nd	(ἐ)λε – λύ – κ – εις	(ἐ)λε – λύ – κ-ειτε
3rd	(ἐ)λε – λύ – κ – ει	(ἐ)λε–λύ–κ-εισαν

(16)   In compound verbs[13], the augment and reduplication are inserted between the preposition and the simple verb.

ἀπεκεφάλισα (Mk 6:16) > ἀπ(ο)-ε-κεφάλι-σ-α
> ἀπό (= *away from*) + κεφαλή (= *head*) + σ + aorist ending

§9   CONTRACTED VERBS

(1)   When the stem of the verb ends in -ε or -α or -ο, contraction takes place in the formation of certain tenses.

(2)   The rules of contraction are as follows:

$$\varepsilon + \varepsilon = \varepsilon\iota$$
$$\varepsilon + o = o\upsilon$$
ε disappears before a long vowel/diphthong

$$\alpha + o/\omega/o\upsilon = \omega$$
$$\alpha + \varepsilon/\eta = \alpha$$
$$\alpha + \varepsilon\iota/\eta = \alpha$$

o + long vowel = ω
o + short vowel = ου
o before ου disappears
any combination of o with ι = οι

(3)   The present indicative active of φιλέω (= *I love*) should be noted:

Person	Singular	Plural
1st	φιλ-ῶ	φιλ-οῦμεν
2nd	φιλ-εῖς	φιλ-εῖτε
3rd	φιλ-εῖ	φιλ-οῦσι(ν)

[13] See 2§11.

(4) τιμάω (= *I honour*) contracts as follows in the present indicative:

1st	τιμ-ῶ	τιμ-ῶμεν
2nd	τιμ-ᾷς	τιμ-ᾶτε
3rd	τιμ-ᾷ	τιμ-ῶσι(ν)

(5) Verbs in -όω contract like δηλόω (= *I make clear, show*).

1st	δηλ- ῶ	δηλ-οῦμεν
2nd	δηλ- οῖς	δηλ-οῦτε
3rd	δηλ- οῖ	δηλ-οῦσι(ν)

§10 FUTURE AND AORIST OF CONTRACTED VERBS

(1) Before forming the future, aorist or perfect of these verbs, the final letter of the stem is lengthened.

(2) To form the future of ποιέω, take the stem ποιε, lengthen the final ε to η , insert σ , then add the endings of the future which are the same as for the present. See Mk 1:17 – ποιήσω = *I shall make.*

(3) Similarly, to form the aorist of ποιέω take the stem ποιε, prefix it with the augment ἐ, lengthen the final ε of the stem to η, insert σ, then add the endings of the aorist. See Mk 3:16 – ἐποίησεν = *he made, appointed.*

(4) εὐδόκησα (Mk 1:11) is aorist from εὐ-δοκέ-ω = *I take delight.* Most English translations render this aorist by a present tense, taking it as a timeless aorist.

(5) καλέω is an exception to the rule. The ε remains short. See Mk 1:20 - ἐκάλεσεν = *he called.*

(6) The α at the end of the stem of πεινάω (= *I am hungry*) remains as α (which can be long as well as short[14]) before the σ of the aorist. See Mk 2:25 – ἐπείνασεν.

---

[14] See 1§12.

(7)   An example of a perfect can be seen in Mk 4:39 –
πεφίμωσο = *be muzzled*. This is 2nd person singular of the
perfect imperative middle or passive of φιμόω. Cf. λέλυσο.
Note the reduplication with π- and not with φ-. This is normal
with an aspirated double letter. Cf. φεύγω, πέφευγα (see
Appendix 2).

§11   COMPOUND VERBS

(1)   Very frequently, a simple verb like λύω is prefixed by a
preposition.[15] This can make the basic meaning of the simple
verb more explicit.

ἀπό = *away from*; ἐπί = *upon;* λύω = *I loose*

ἀπο-λύω = *I release, set free, send away* [Mk 6:36; 8:3,9]

ἐπι-λύω = *I explain* [Mk 4:34.]

(2)   In certain cases, the meaning of the preposition is clearly
seen to be carried over into the compound verb.

ἐκ = *out of*; ἀμφί = *around*; ἐπί = *upon*; βάλλω = *I throw*

ἐκ-βάλλω = *I throw out, drive out* [Mk 1:12]

ἀμφι-βάλλω = *I throw around, cast* [a net – Mk 1:16]

ἐπι-βάλλω = *I throw upon, place upon* [Mk 4:37; 11:7]

(3)   This can also be seen in compound verbs of coming or
going.

εἰς = *into*; ἐκ/ἐξ = *out of*; ἔρχομαι[16] = *I come, go*

εἰσ-έρχομαι = *I go in, enter* [Mk 1:21; 2:1; 3:1]

ἐξ-έρχομαι = *I go out* [Mk 1:25]

[15] See 3§15.

[16] See 6§4(3).

(4) Similarly, βαίνω = *I come, go*. This is never found as a simple verb, but only in compounds.

Since ἀνά = *up* and κατά = *down*, ἀναβαίνω = *I come up* and καταβαίνω = *I come down*. These verbs are used in Mk 1:10 of Jesus *coming up* out of the water at his baptism and of the Holy Spirit *coming down* upon him.

(5) The **augment** in compound verbs is placed between the preposition and the simple verb.

ἐπέλυεν = ἐπί + ε (augment) + λυ (stem) + εν
(imperfect ending)

Mk 4:34 - τοῖς μαθηταῖς ἐπέλυεν πάντα
He used to explain all things to the disciples.

(6) διακονέω = *I serve* is not a compound verb. Compare the cognate noun ὁ/ἡ διάκονος = *the servant*. Yet this verb behaves as if it were a compound in the formation of past tenses. It lengthens -α- to -η- instead of prefixing ἐ-.

διηκόνουν = διακονε + ον (3rd person plural imperfect)
[Mk 1:13]
Note that this verb takes the dative case.

διηκόνει = διακόνε + ε (3rd person singular imperfect)
[Mk 1:31]

ASSIGNMENTS

1. **STUDY** carefully the table of the Regular Greek Verb (see Appendix 1), noting the six tenses, the six moods and the three voices.

2. **LEARN** the paradigms for the six tenses of the indicative active of λύω.

ACTIVE

		Present	Future	Imper.
Singular	1.	λύω	λύσω	ἔλυον
	2.	λύεις	λύσεις	ἔλυες
	3.	λύει	λύσει	ἔλυε(ν)
Plural	1.	λύομεν	λύσομεν	ἐλύομεν
	2.	λύετε	λύσετε	ἐλύετε
	3.	λύουσι(ν)	λύσουσι(ν)	ἔλυον

		Aorist	Perf.	Plprf.
Singular	1.	ἔλυσα	λέλυκα	ἐλελύκειν
	2.	ἔλυσας	λέλυκας	ἐλελύκεις
	3.	ἔλυσε(ν)	λέλυκε(ν)	ἐλελύκει
Plural	1.	ἐλύσαμεν	λελύκαμεν	ἐλελύκειμεν
	2.	ἐλύσατε	λελύκατε	ἐλελύκειτε
	3.	ἔλυσαν	λελύκασι(ν)	ἐλελύκεισαν

3. **LEARN** the following Greek verbs:

	Meaning	Mark
ἀκούω	I hear	2:1,17; 3:8,21; 4:3,9, κτλ
βάλλω	I throw	2:22; 4:26; 7:27
βαπτίζω	I baptize	1:4,5,8,9
γράφω	I write	1:2
διδάσκω	I teach	1:21,22
ἐσθίω	I eat	1:6; 2:16
εὑρίσκω	I find	1:37; 7:30
ἔχω	I have	1:22,32; 2:10,17,19; κτλ
κηρύσσω	I proclaim	1:4,7,14,38,39
λέγω	I speak	1:7,15,30,37,38,40,41,44
πέμπω	I send	5:12
πιστεύω	I believe	1:15
σώζω[17]	I save	3:4
φέρω	I carry	1:32; 5:34

---

[17] Occasionally, you will find an iota subscript in the stem of this verb: σῴζω (see UBSD 177a); ἐσῴζοντο (Mk 6:56).

4.   **TRANSLATE** into English:

(1)   ἐβάπτισα (Mk 1:8)
(2)   βαπτίσει (Mk 1:8)[18]
(3)   ἐκήρυσσεν (Mk 1:7)
(4)   ἐκβάλλει (Mk 1:12)
(5)   ἐδίδασκεν (Mk 1:21)
(6)   λέγουσιν (Mk 1:30,37)
(7)   ἔφερον (Mk 1:32)
(8)   σέσωκεν (Mk 5:34)
(9)   ἤκουσεν (Mk 6:14)

5.   **TRANSLATE** into Greek:
(1)   You (singular) are eating.
(2)   He is speaking.
(3)   They will loose.
(4)   You (plural) were hearing.
(5)   They used to write (imperfect tense).
(6)   I have written.

6.   **RE-READ** carefully §§9 and 10

7.   **LEARN** the following contracted verbs found in Mark.

	Meaning	Contracted	Uncontracted
βοάω	I shout out	βοῶντος (1:3)	βοάοντος

= of one shouting, crying out (present participle)[19]

ποιέω	I make, do	ποιεῖτε (1:3)	ποιέετε

= you are making (pres.indic.) or make (pres.imper.)[20]

[18] Note that before the ending the δ sound in ζ falls out, leaving σ on its own in the future and the aorist tenses of βαπτίζω.

[19] See Chapters 7 and 8.

[20] We shall be studying the imperative mood in Chapter Seven. Meantime, note that the 2nd person plural of the present imperative active is identical in form with the 2nd person plural of present indicative active.

8. **TRANSLATE** into Greek:

(1) You (singular) are shouting out.
(2) He is making.
(3) You (plural) are doing.
(4) They called.[21]

9. **STUDY CAREFULLY** the following examples of contracted verbs found in Mark and **WRITE DOWN** their uncontracted forms.

(1) -έω contraction:

From ποιέω = *I make, do*:	ποιεῖτε (Mk 1:3; 7:13)
From περιπατέω = *I walk about*:	περιπατοῦσιν (Mk 7:5)
From λαλέω = *I speak*:	λαλεῖν (Mk 7:37)
From ζητέω = *I seek*:	ζητεῖ (Mk 8:12)
From ἀκολουθέω = *I follow*:	ἠκολούθουν (Mk 2:15)

(2) -άω contraction:

From τιμάω = *I honour*:   τίμα (Imperative[22] = *honour*)

(3) -όω contraction:

From κοινόω = *make common, defile*: κοινοῖ (Mk 7:20,23)

10. **RE-READ** carefully §8(16) and §11 on **compound verbs**.

11. If ἀπό = *away* and ἡ κεφαλή = *the head*,
           what does ἀπεκεφάλισα (Mk 6:16) mean?

If you have difficulty in working this out, notice that ἔλυσα in Appendix 1 is the aorist indicative active of λύω = *I loosed*.

[21] See 2§10(5).

[22] See 7§2(2).

CHAPTER THREE

Greek Nouns

§1   INFLECTION of NOUNS in ENGLISH

(1)   **English nouns** have only the remnants of a case system.

(2)   The **plural number** is usually designated by the addition of the letter -s or the letters -es, as, for example, in book/books or leaf/leaves or box/boxes. There are irregular plural formations, as, for example, man/men, woman/women, child/children.

(3)   Apart from these indications of the plural, the only other remaining indication of case is in the **genitive** or **possessive** case, which is designated by -'s or -s'; thus, the man's (for manes) house or the children's books or the students' union.

§2   INFLECTION of GREEK NOUNS

(1)   **Greek is very much more highly inflected**, for nouns as well as for verbs. The **Greek noun** has **five cases** – nominative, vocative, accusative, genitive, dative. There is no ablative case in Greek. The functions of the Latin ablative are taken over by other cases, especially the genitive and the dative, sometimes with the help of prepositions.

(2)   These cases are found both in the singular and in the plural number[1].

---

[1] In classical Greek, there was a third number – the dual – used when referring to two people or things. This had fallen out of use by the time of Hellenistic Greek.

(3)   Greek nouns are declined or decline – from the Latin **declinare** = *to bend*; or from Greek κλίνω = *I bend*.

§3   DECLENSION

(1)   The **case of a noun** indicates its relation to other words in the clause.

(2)   The **declension** is its deviation from the upright, if one considers the nominative to be the perpendicular.

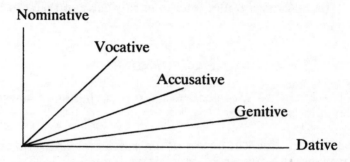

(3)   The **nominative case** is the case of the subject of the verb or clause or sentence. In the English sentence, *The apostle, O friend, brings the good news of God to the people, the apostle* is the subject and would go into the nominative case in Greek – ὁ ἀπόστολος.

(4)   The **vocative case** is the case of address. In English, and sometimes also in Greek, it is preceded by *O* – Greek ὦ – *O friend* = ὦ φίλε.

(5)   The **accusative** is the case of the object of a clause. In our sentence in (3), *the good news* is what is brought by the subject of the clause – *the apostle*. So it goes into the accusative case in Greek – τὸ εὐαγγέλιον.[2]

(6)   The **genitive case** denotes a variety of relationships,

[2] As we shall see later, the nominative, vocative and accusative of neuter nouns are identical.

including possession – as in our sentence in (3), where *of God* indicates the possessor of the good news – τοῦ Θεοῦ.[3]

(7)　The **dative case** is the case of the indirect object. In our sentence it indicates the persons to whom or for whom the good news is being given – *to* or *for the people* = τῷ λαῷ.

(8)　Our sentence is an example of an English sentence containing all five Greek cases: *The apostle, O friend, brings (or is bringing) the good news of God to the people.*

ὁ ἀπόστολος, ὦ φίλε, φέρει τὸ εὐαγγέλιον τοῦ Θεοῦ τῷ λαῷ.
ho apostolos, o file, ferei to euangelion tou theou to lao.

§4　GENDER

(1)　There are three genders in Greek, as in English: masculine, feminine and neuter.

(2)　As in English, names of male human beings and animals are masculine; those of females are feminine.

(3)　However, many nouns which would be regarded as neuter in English are masculine or feminine in Greek. Abstract nouns, for example, are usually feminine in Greek.

§5　AGREEMENT in NUMBER

(1)　As in English, the verb usually agrees in number with the subject of the clause, whether that subject be a noun or a pronoun. A singular noun or pronoun takes a verb in the 3rd person singular, while a plural noun or pronoun normally takes a verb in the 3rd person plural.

---

[3] Other uses of the genitive case will be noted as we come to them. See 3§13(3), 3§14, 4§13(3), 8§8(2).

(2) Neuter plural nouns and pronouns, however, usually take a 3rd person singular verb.[4]

ἄλλα πλοῖα ἦν μετ' αὐτοῦ. (Mk 4:36)

[ἦν is the 3rd person singular of the imperfect indicative active of εἰμί = *I am*. So ἦν = *he/she/it was*.]

Other ships were with him.

τὰ κύματα ἐπέβαλλεν εἰς τὸ πλοῖον. (Mk 4:37)
The waves were beating against the ship.

§6 THE INDEFINITE PRONOUN

(1) In English, there is an indefinite article – *a* or *an* (before a vowel). Thus, *a book* or *an apple*.

(2) In Greek, there is no indefinite article. The absence of a definite article indicates that the noun is to be translated into English either on its own or with the indefinite article. Thus, *book* or *a book; apple* or *an apple*.

(3) There is **an indefinite pronoun**, which is the equivalent of *someone, something, anyone, anything, a certain person*, κτλ. .

	Masculine	Feminine	Neuter
		SINGULAR	
Nom.	τις	τις	τι
Acc.	τινα	τινα	τι
Gen.	τινος	τινος	τινος
Dat.	τινι	τινι	τινι

---

[4] In classical Greek, a neuter plural subject always had a singular verb. This rule is usually broken in the New Testament with neuter words used in a personal sense; e.g., τέκνα, δαιμόνια and sometimes πνεύματα. See Mk 1:27; 3:11. In Mt. 10:29, δύο στρουθία has a singular verb, but in Lk. 12:6, πέντε στρουθία has a plural verb, perhaps to stress that even the one sparrow thrown into the bargain is not forgotten by God.

PLURAL

Nom.	τινες	τινες	τινα
Acc.	τινας	τινας	τινα
Gen.	τινων	τινων	τινων
Dat.	τισι(ν)	τισι(ν)	τισι(ν)

(4) This is exactly the same as for the interrogative pronoun
= *who*? *what*? – except that the interrogative always has an
acute accent on the first syllable – τίς; τί; κτλ. .

Τίνα με λέγουσιν οἱ ἄνθρωποι εἶναι; (Mk 8:27)

[Notice that the "subject" of the infinitive in Greek is in the
accusative case.]

Who do people say that I am?

[*Who* not *whom* in English since *who* is the complement after
the verb *to be*.]

(5) The indefinite pronoun never has an accent on the first
syllable and is enclitic, that is, it throws its accent back to the
preceding word, which then can have an acute accent on the
final syllable.

Εἴ τις θέλει ὀπίσω μου ἐλθεῖν . . . .(Mk 8:34)

If anyone wishes to come after me . . . .

§7 THE DEFINITE ARTICLE

(1) The definite article should be learnt by heart as soon as
possible. LEARN it across the line – nom. sing. masc., fem.,
and neuter; then acc. sing., masc., fem., and neuter; κτλ. .

	Masculine	*Feminine*	*Neuter*
		SINGULAR	
Nom.	ὁ	ἡ	τό
Acc.	τόν	τήν	τό
Gen.	τοῦ	τῆς	τοῦ
Dat.	τῷ	τῇ	τῷ

PLURAL

Nom.	οἱ	αἱ	τά
Acc.	τούς	τάς	τά
Gen.	τῶν	τῶν	τῶν
Dat.	τοῖς	ταῖς	τοῖς

(2) **The definite article must agree with its noun in gender, number and case.**

(3) **Notice that the acute accent changes to grave when the article is followed by another Greek word. Cf. 4§14(4).**

§8   THREE DECLENSIONS

(1)   Nouns which are declined in a similar way belong to the same **declension**.

(2)   There are **three declensions** into which all Greek nouns are grouped depending on the way in which they are declined.

	MASCULINE	FEMININE	NEUTER
Article	ὁ	ἡ	τό
Declension			
1st α/η	-ας/-ης νεανίας *youth* προφήτης	-α/-α/-η δόξα *glory* ἡμέρα *day* ἀρχή *beginning*	*NONE*
2nd ο	-ος λόγος *word*	-ος only a few ἔρημος *desert* ὁδός *way* παρθένος *virgin*	-ον ἔργον
3rd genitive in -ος	φύλαξ *guard* φύλακος σάλπιγξ *trumpet* σάλπιγγος	ἐλπίς ἐλπίδος *hope*	γράμμα γράμματος *letter of* *alphabet*

§9 FIRST DECLENSION FEMININE NOUNS

(1) **Feminine Nouns** in the first declension end in α or η.

(2) The various endings of three such nouns should be studied carefully, compared with the endings of the feminine article and **LEARNED BY HEART**. ἡ ἀρχή[5] = *the beginning*; ἡ ἡμέρα = *the day;* ἡ δόξα = *glory*.

	Singular	Plural	Singular	Plural	Singular	Plural
Nom.	ἀρχή	ἀρχαί	ἡμέρα	ἡμέραι	δόξα	δόξαι
Voc.	ἀρχή	ἀρχαί	ἡμέρα	ἡμέραι	δόξα	δόξαι
Acc.	ἀρχήν	ἀρχάς	ἡμέραν	ἡμερας	δόξαν	δόξας
Gen.	ἀρχῆς	ἀρχῶν	ἡμέρας	ἡμερῶν	δόξης	δοξῶν
Dat.	ἀρχῇ	ἀρχαῖς	ἡμέρᾳ	ἡμέραις	δόξῃ	δόξαις

(3) The vocative (singular and plural) in all these feminine first declension nouns is the same as the nominative (singular and plural).

(4) The singular endings of nouns whose stems end in a vowel or ϱ retain α throughout. They are α pure, like ἡμέρα. Those whose stems end in a consonant change from α to η for the genitive and dative. They are α impure, like δόξα.

(5) The genitive plural of all first declension nouns ends in -ῶν, which is a contraction of -άων.[6]

§10 FIRST DECLENSION MASCULINE NOUNS

(1) There are a few masculine nouns in the first declension ending in -ης and -ας. They are declined as follows:

---

[5] ἀρχή is used in Mk 1:1 without the definite article since the verse is a heading or title either to the prologue or to the whole gospel.

[6] See J.H.Moulton, *Grammar of New Testament Greek*, vol.2, p.117.

	Singular	Plural	Singular	Plural
Nom.	προφήτης	προφῆται	νεανίας	νεανίαι
Voc.	προφῆτα	προφῆται	νεανία	νεανίαι
Acc.	προφήτην	προφήτας	νεανίαν	νεανίας
Gen.	προφήτου	προφητῶν	νεανίου	νεανιῶν
Dat.	προφήτῃ	προφήταις	νεανίᾳ	νεανίαις

(2) The vocàtive singular of these masculine nouns is different from the nominative singular.

(3) The genitive singular ends in -ου.

(4) νεανίας like ἡμέρα is α pure and retains α in the dative singular, though not in the genitive.

(5) The masculine plural endings are the same as those for the feminine plural endings.

§11 SECOND DECLENSION NOUNS

(1) The characteristic of the second declension nouns is o in the ending of the nominative singular, whether they be masculine in -ος or neuter in -ον. Thus, ὁ λόγος = *the word;* and τὸ ἔργον = *the deed, the action, work.*

(2) They are declined as follows:

	Singular	Plural	Singular	Plural
Nom.	λόγος	λόγοι	ἔργον	ἔργα
Voc.	λόγε	λόγοι	ἔργον	ἔργα
Acc.	λόγον	λόγους	ἔργον	ἔργα
Gen.	λόγου	λόγων	ἔργου	ἔργων
Dat.	λόγῳ	λόγοις	ἔργῳ	ἔργοις

(3) Most second declension nouns in -ος are masculine; but there are a few that are feminine: e.g.,

ἡ ἔρημος = *the desert*   ἡ ὁδός = *the way*
ἡ (or ὁ) παρθένος = *the virgin*   ἡ τρίβος = *the path.*

Three of these occur in Mk 1:3.

(4)   Second declension nouns in -ov are neuter.

(5)   As usual with neuter nouns and adjectives, nominative, vocative and accusative are identical in singular as in plural.

§12   THIRD DECLENSION

(1)   **Third declension** nouns have the following case endings

	MASC./FEM.	NEUT.	MASC./FEM.	NEUT.
	SINGULAR		PLURAL	
Nom.	-ς	None	-ες	-α
Voc.	-	None	-ες	-α
Acc.	-α (-ν)	None	-ας	-α
Gen.	-ος (-ως)		-ων	
Dat.	-ι		-σι(ν)	

(2)   Since the nominative singular has various endings and since the stem can be found only by taking off the genitive singular case ending, it is necessary to learn not only the nominative singular but also the genitive singular of third declension nouns as well as their gender, indicated in the lexicon by means of the definite article.

(3)   Some paradigms:

	Masculine	Feminine	Neuter
	ὁ φύλαξ	ἡ ἐλπίς	τὸ γράμμα
	the guard	*hope*	*the letter*
			(of alphabet)

	Singular	**Plural**
Nom.	φύλαξ	φύλακες
Voc.	φύλαξ	φύλακες
Acc.	φύλακα	φύλακας
Gen.	φύλακος	φυλάκων
Dat.	φύλακι	φύλαξι(ν)

Masculine	Feminine	Neuter
Nom.	ἐλπίς	ἐλπίδες
Voc.	ἐλπίς	ἐλπίδες
Acc.	ἐλπίδα	ἐλπίδας
Gen.	ἐλπίδος	ἐλπίδων
Dat.	ἐλπίδι	ἐλπίσι(ν)
Nom.	γράμμα	γράμματα
Voc.	γράμμα	γράμματα
Acc.	γράμμα	γράμματα
Gen.	γράμματος	γράμματων
Dat.	γράμματι	γράμμασι(ν)

(4) The characteristic of the third declension is the genitive ending in -ος or -ως in certain instances.

(5) In order to discover the stem, take off the ending of the genitive singular.

(6) Other cases, apart from the nominative and the vocative, are formed by adding the correct endings to the stem.

(7) There are a few neuter nouns in the third declension which have a stem ending in -εσ-. In the genitive singular, the final -σ- of the stem dropped out between the two vowels and contraction took place; e.g.,

τὸ γένος = *the race* – gen.: τοῦ γένεσος > γένους[7]

τὸ ἔθνος, ἔθνους = *the nation*

τὸ ὄρος, ὄρους = *the mountain.*

All these neuter nouns have nom./voc./accus. plural in -εσα > -η.

(8) **Relationship Nouns of Third Declension** require to be specially noted.

---

[7] > = *becomes* or *contracts to*. The σ falls out and ε+ο = ου by one of the rules of contraction [see 2§9(2)].

ὁ πατήρ   ἡ μήτηρ   ἡ θυγάτηρ   ὁ ἀνήρ = the
= the father = the mother = the daughter man/husband

Singular

Nom.	πατήρ	μήτηρ	θυγάτηρ	ἀνήρ
Voc.	πάτερ		θύγατερ	ἄνερ
Acc.	πατέρα	μητέρα	θυγατέρα	ἄνδρα
Gen.	πατρός	μητρός	θυγατρός	ἀνδρός
Dat.	πατρί	μητρί	θυγατρί	ἀνδρί

Plural

Nom.	πατέρες	μητέρες	θυγατέρες	ἄνδρες
Voc.	πατέρες	μητέρες	θυγατέρες	ἄνδρες
Acc.	πατέρας	μητέρας	θυγατέρας	ἄνδρας
Gen.	πατέρων	μητέρων	θυγατέρων	ἀνδρῶν
Dat.	πατράσι(ν)	μητράσι(ν)	θυγατράσι(ν)ἀνδράσι(ν)	

(9)   Some common third declension nouns found in Mk 1 to 8:

Mark

ὁ ἄρχων, ἄρχοντος *ruler*
    τῷ ἄρχοντι   3:22 (dat. singular)
ὁ βασιλεύς, βασιλεύς *king*   6:14,22,26,27
    τὸν βασιλέα   6:25 (accus. singular)
ὁ ἰχθύς, ἰχθύος *fish*
    τοὺς ἰχθύας   6:38,41 (accus. plural)
    τῶν ἰχθύων   6:43 (gen. plural)
ὁ πατήρ, πατρός *father*
    τὸν πατέρα   1:20; 5:40; 7:10 (accus. singular)
    τοῦ πατρός   8:38 (gen. singular)
    τῷ πατρί   7:11,12 (dat. singular)
ὁ πούς, ποδός *foot*
    τοὺς πόδας   5:22, 7:25 (accus. plural)
    τῶν ποδῶν   6:11 (gen. plural)
ἡ γυνή, γυναικός *woman,*   5:25, 33; 7:25, 26
                    wife
    τὴν γυναῖκα   6:17,18 (accus. singular)
ἡ θρίξ, τριχός *hair*
    τὰς τρίχας   1:6 (accus. plural)
ἡ θυγάτηρ, θυγατρός   5:34, 35
                    daughter
    τῆς θυγατρός   6:22, 7:26, 29 (gen. singular)

ἡ νύξ, νυκτός *night*
τὴν νύκτα	4:27 (accus. singular)
τῆς νυκτός	5:5, 6:48 (gen. singular)

ἡ πόλις, πόλεως *city* — 1:33,45
τὴν πόλιν	1:45; 5:14[8] (accus. singular)
τὰς πόλεις	6:56 (accus. plural)
τῶν πόλεων	6:33 (gen. plural)

ἡ χείρ, χειρός *hand*
τὴν χεῖρα	1:41, 3:1,3,5 (accus. singular)
τῆς χειρός	1:31 (gen. singular)

τὸ αἷμα, αἵματος *blood*	5:25,29 (gen. singular)
τὸ γένος, γένους	
(from γένεσος) *race*	
τῷ γένει	7:26 (dat. singular)
τὸ ὄνομα, ὀνόματος *name*	3:16,17; 5:9, 6:14
τῷ ὀνόματι	5:22 (dat. singular)
τὸ ὄρος, ὄρους	
(from ὄρεσος) *mountain*	3:13; 6:46
τῷ ὄρει	5:11 (dat. singular)
τοῖς ὄρεσιν	5:5 (dat. plural)
τὸ οὖς, ὠτός *ear*	
τὰ ὦτα	4:23 (accus. plural)
τὸ πνεῦμα, πνεύματος *spirit*	1:10,12
τῷ πνεύματι	1:8,23; 2:8
τοῖς πνεύμασι	1:27 (dat. plural)
τὸ σῶμα, σώματος *body*	
τῷ σώματι	5:29 (dat. singular)
τὸ ὕδωρ, ὕδατος *water*	
τῷ ὕδατι	1:8 (dat. singular)
τοῦ ὕδατος	1:10 (gen. singular)

§13 EXPRESSING SPACE and TIME

(1)   The cases of nouns were originally used to express all the relations within a sentence or clause – whether they were local, temporal or other relations. The accusative case denoted

---

[8] The ancient Greek city of Byzantium became the πόλις of Constantine (*Constantinople*) in A.D.330 and then *Istanbul* (εἰς τὴν πόλιν = *into the city*).

extension or motion towards. The genitive case expressed separation or motion away from. The dative case was used to indicate rest at or upon, place where and also instrument.

(2) Certain temporal indications can be given by case alone. **Extent/duration of time/time how long** can be expressed by the accusative case.

τεσσαράκοντα ἡμέρας (Mk 1:13)
during/for forty days

(3)   **Time within which** can be indicated by the simple genitive case, though the preposition ἐπί came to be used along with the genitive.

νυκτὸς καὶ ἡμέρας (Mk 5:5)
night and day

Note that the preceding phrase (διὰ παντός = *continually* – see UBSD 41b) does not agree with either of these nouns in the genitive, both of which are feminine. Which gender is παντός?[9]

ἐπὶ 'Αβιαθὰρ ἀρχιερέως (Mk 2:26)
In the days of/time of Abiathar as high priest

(4)   **Time when/point of time** can be expressed by means of the simple dative though the preposition ἐν can also be used.

ἐν τοῖς σάββασιν (Mk 2:23)
τοῖς σάββασιν (Mk 2:24)
on the Sabbath.

§14   PRICE or VALUE

The genitive case is also used to express **cost** or **price** or **value**.

δηναρίων διακοσίων ἄρτους (Mk 6:37)
loaves worth 200 denarii[10]

[9] See 4§9.

[10] Since a *denarius* was a working man's wages for a day, 200 would have been far in excess of the £20 suggested by the New English Bible.

§15 PREPOSITIONS

(1)   With the development of the language, adverbs came to be placed before nouns and pronouns to give greater precision and so to make the meaning clearer. Thus, the function of the cases was extended by means of these parts of speech placed before the nouns or pronouns and so named prepositions, from the Latin verb **prae-ponere** = *to place before.*

(2)   Prepositions are said loosely to govern cases of nouns, though it is really the noun (or pronoun) that is the governing element in the prepositional expression.

(3)   Some prepositions govern one case, some two cases and others three cases. The meaning differs according to the case that is governed. Each preposition has a basic meaning and also extended meanings.

(4)   Prepositions ending in a vowel (except πρό and περί) elide the final vowel before a word beginning with a vowel - ἀνά, ἀντί, ἀπό, διά, ἐπί, κατά, μετά, παρά, ὑπό.

(5)   The following prepositions govern one case:

		Mark (first 5)
ἀντί with genitive	*instead of*	10:45
ἀπό with genitive	*away from*	1:9,42; 2:20,21; 3:7
εἰς with accusative	*into*	1:4,9,10,12,14
ἐκ/ἐξ with genitive	*from, out of*	1:10,11,25,26,29
ἐν with dative	*in, on, among, within, by means of*	1:2,3,4,5,8
πρό with genitive	*before*	1:2
σύν with dative	*with, together with*	2:26; 4:10; 8:34

(6)   Note the difference between ἀπό (*away from the outside of something*); and ἐκ (*out of the inside of something*).

ἀναβαίνων ἐκ τοῦ ὕδατος . . . (Mk 1:10)
coming up out of the water . . .

εἰσῆλθεν εἰς οἶκον ἀπὸ τοῦ ὄχλου. (Mk 7:17)
He went into a house away from the crowd.

(7) Note also the distinction between εἰς (motion into); and
ἐν (rest in or on).

φωνὴ βοῶντος ἐν τῇ ἐρήμῳ . . . . (Mk 1:3)
A voice of one crying in the desert

καὶ εὐθὺς τὸ πνεῦμα αὐτὸν ἐκβάλλει εἰς τὴν ἔρημον.
(Mk 1:12)
And immediately the Spirit throws him out into the desert.[11]

(8) Certain prepositions govern two cases:

			Mark (first 5)
διά	with accusative	*on account of, because of*	2:4,18,27; 3:9; 4:5
	with genitive	*through*	2:1,23;5:5;6:2; 7:31
	Note: δι' ἡμερῶν	*through days, several days afterwards*	2:1
κατά	with accusative	*down towards, according to*	

Note special idiomatic phrases:

κατ' ἐξουσίαν	*with authority*	1:27
κατ' ἰδίαν	*privately*	4:34; 6:31,32; 7:33
κατὰ τὴν παραδόσιν τῶν πρεσβυτέρων		7:5
according to the tradition of the elders		
κατὰ μόνας	*alone*	4:10
καθ' ἡμέραν	*daily, every day*	14:49

	with genitive	*down from, against*	5:13 3:6
μετά	with accusative	*after*	1:14; 8:31
	with genitive	*with*	1:13,20,29,36; 2:16
περί	with accusative	*about*	1:6; 3:8,32,34; 4:10
	with genitive	*concerning*	1:30,44; 5:16,27; 7:6

---

[11] Notice here, and frequently in Mark, the use of the present tense where
in English we would have to use a past tense. This is known as the *historic
present.*

πρός	with accusative	*towards*	1:5,27,32,33,40
	with dative	*near*	5:11
ὑπέρ	with accusative	*above*	none in Mark
	with genitive	*on behalf of*	9:40; 14:24
ὑπό	with accusative	*under*	4:21,32
	with genitive	*by*	1:5,9,13;2:3; 5:4

(9) Other prepositions govern three cases:

ἐπί	with accusative	*up on to*	2:14,21;3:24,25,26
	with genitive	*upon,*	2:10; 4:1,26,31;6:47
		in the days of	2:26
	with dative	(rest) *upon*	1:22,45;3:5;6:25,28
παρά	with accusative	(motion to)	
		beside	1:16; 2:13; 4:1,4,15
	with genitive	(motion)	
		from beside	3:21; 5:26; 8:11
	with dative	(rest) *beside*	10:27

(10) Note Mk 3:21 – οἱ παρ' αὐτοῦ – *his friends* (RSV 1st ed.), *his family* (RSV 2nd ed., NEB)

Vincent Taylor, p.236: "The family at Nazareth, and not merely *his friends* [RV], are indicated." Do you agree with this view?

(11) Certain prepositions can never be used as prefixes in compound verbs. Those found in Mark with the genitive case are

ἔμπροσθεν	*in front of*
ἕνεκα	*for the sake of*
ἔξω	*outside of*
ἔσω	*within*
ὀπίσω	*behind*
πέραν	*beyond*
πλήν	*except*
χωρίς	*apart from*

Thus, ἔμπροσθεν πάντων (Mk 2:12)
ἔξω τῆς χώρας (Mk 5:10)
ὀπίσω μου (Mk 1:7)
πέραν τοῦ 'Ιορδάνου (Mk 3:8)
χωρὶς παραβολῆς (Mk.4:34)

Can you translate all these prepositional phrases?

§16 SOME COMMON GREEK PREPOSITIONS

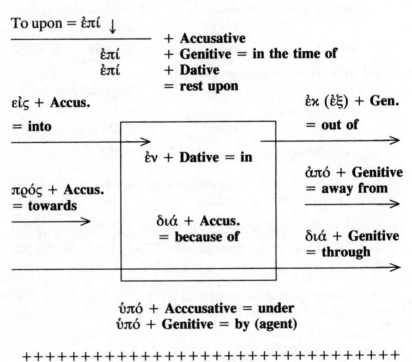

To upon = ἐπί ↓
              + Accusative
      ἐπί   + Genitive = in the time of
      ἐπί   + Dative
               = rest upon

εἰς + Accus.   ἐκ (ἐξ) + Gen.

= into   = out of

           ἐν + Dative = in

                              ἀπό + Genitive
πρός + Accus.   = away from
= towards

           διά + Accus.
           = because of   διά + Genitive
                            = through

ὑπό + Acccusative = under
ὑπό + Genitive = by (agent)

+++

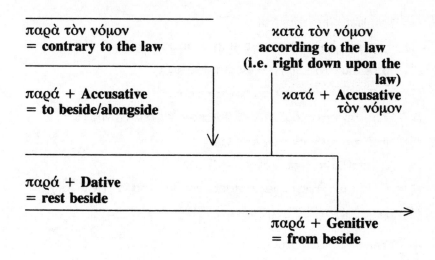

παρὰ τὸν νόμον
= contrary to the law

παρά + Accusative
= to beside/alongside

κατὰ τὸν νόμον
according to the law
(i.e. right down upon the
law)
κατά + Accusative
τὸν νόμον

παρά + Dative
= rest beside

παρά + Genitive
= from beside

ASSIGNMENTS

1. **WRITE DOWN and LEARN** all the Greek words found in this lesson. As far as third declension nouns are concerned, remember to learn the article as well as the genitive singular.

2. Write down and learn the following words, all of which occur in Mk 1:

Nouns		*Verbs*	
ὁ ἄγγελος	messenger	ἀποστέλλω	send
ἡ ἀρχή	beginning	βοάω	shout, cry out
ἡ ἔρημος	desert	γράφω	write
τὸ εὐαγγέλιον	good news	ἑτοιμάζω	make ready
ὁ Θεός	God	κατασκευάζω	prepare
ὁ κύριος	lord, master	ποιέω	make, do
ὁ λόγος	word		
ἡ ὁδός	road		
τὸ πρόσωπον	face		
ὁ προφήτης	prophet		
ἡ τρίβος	path		
ὁ υἱός	son		
ἡ φωνή	voice		

3. Translate into English:

(1) γράφεις τοὺς λόγους τοῦ προφήτου.

(2) διδάσκει τὸ εὐαγγέλιον τοῦ Θεοῦ.

(3) ὁ Κύριος ἀποστέλλει τὸν ἄγγελον.

(4) Τὸ σάββατον διὰ τὸν ἄνθρωπον ἐγένετο. (Mk 2:27)

(5) ὑπὸ τὴν κλίνην . (Mk 4:21)

(6) ἐβαπτίζοντο ὑπ' αὐτοῦ. (Mk 1:5)[12]

(7) ὁ 'Ιησοῦς ἀνεχώρησεν πρὸς τὴν θάλασσαν. (Mk 3:7)

(8) λέγουσιν αὐτῷ περὶ αὐτῆς. (Mk 1:30)

4. Translate into Greek:

(1) I am preparing the way of the Lord.

(2) The prophet is writing the good news.

(3) God is sending out the messengers.

(4) We shall make ready the paths in the desert.

(5) A voice is shouting to the son.

(6) She is writing the beginning of the gospel of God.

5. **READ** carefully the Greek text of Mk 1:1-3. There are 16 nouns in these verses. Which 2 are in the nominative case, which 4 are in the accusative case, which 7 are in the genitive case, and which 3 are in the dative?

6. **EXPLAIN** the reason for the case of each noun. Is it because it is the subject or the object of the verb in its clause? Or is it possessive? Or is it following a preposition? Write down the nominative singular of each noun along with the definite article and the meaning.

Thus, ἡ αρχή   *the beginning*
        τὸ εὐαγγέλιον   *the good news*
        κτλ.

---

[12] For the pronoun in this sentence and in (8), see 4§10.

Don't worry too much about accents but do remember to put in the rough or smooth breathings whenever a word begins with a vowel or a diphthong.

7. There are three 2nd declension feminine nouns ending in -ος in these verses. In each case, write down the nominative singular along with the definite article. See Chapter 3§11(3).

8. **READ** carefully through the Greek text of Mk 2:23–28. Identify and explain all the prepositions and the cases of the accompanying nouns or pronouns.

CHAPTER FOUR

Greek Adjectives

§1   WHAT IS AN ADJECTIVE?

(1)   As in English, adjectives are used in Greek to describe nouns more fully.

(2)   When they describe nouns, or attribute qualities to them, they are said to be attributive adjectives or to be in attributive position. For example, in *the black cow*, *black* is describing *the cow* or attributing **blackness** to it.

(3)   An adjective can also be used as part of the predicate or verb. Thus, in *The cow is black* or *black is the cow*, *black* is used along with the verb *to be* as part of the predicate. The verb *to be* can be omitted in such a sentence in Greek – *black the cow* or *the cow black*. Such an adjective is said to be in **predicative position** in Greek.

§2   DECLENSION OF ADJECTIVES

(1)   Many adjectives have three terminations, employing the same endings as 2nd declension nouns for the masculine and the neuter and the same endings as 1st declension nouns in -η for the feminine.

(2)   Here is the paradigm for **Adjectives** of the **Second and First Declensions** – ἀγαθός *good*:

	Singular			**Plural**		
	Masc.	**Fem.**	**Neut.**	**Masc.**	**Fem.**	**Neut.**
Nom.	ἀγαθός	ἀγαθή	ἀγαθόν	ἀγαθοί	ἀγαθαί	ἀγαθά
Voc.	ἀγαθέ	ἀγαθή	ἀγαθόν	ἀγαθοί	ἀγαθαί	ἀγαθά
Acc.	ἀγαθόν	ἀγαθήν	ἀγαθόν	ἀγαθούς	ἀγαθάς	ἀγαθά
Gen.	ἀγαθοῦ	ἀγαθῆς	ἀγαθοῦ	ἀγαθῶν	ἀγαθῶν	ἀγαθῶν
Dat.	ἀγαθῷ	ἀγαθῇ	ἀγαθῷ	ἀγαθοῖς	ἀγαθαῖς	ἀγαθοῖς

(3) Where the feminine has α pure, the feminine endings are the same as for ἡμέρα – ἅγιος *holy*.

	Singular			**Plural**		
	Masc.	**Fem.**	**Neut.**	**Masc.**	**Fem.**	**Neut.**
Nom.	ἅγιος	ἁγία	ἅγιον	ἅγιοι	ἅγιαι	ἅγια
Voc.	ἅγιε	ἁγία	ἅγιον	ἅγιοι	ἅγιαι	ἅγια
Acc.	ἅγιον	ἁγίαν	ἅγιον	ἁγίους	ἁγίας	ἅγια
Gen.	ἁγίου	ἁγίας	ἁγίου	ἁγίων	ἁγιῶν	ἁγίων
Dat.	ἁγίῳ	ἁγίᾳ	ἁγίῳ	ἁγίοις	ἁγίαις	ἁγίοις

(4) Adjectives of the **Third Declension** have the same endings for the masculine and the feminine – ἀληθής *true*.

	Singular		**Plural**	
	Masc./Fem.	**Neut.**	**Masc./Fem.**	**Neut.**
Nom.	ἀληθής	ἀληθές	ἀληθεῖς	ἀληθῆ
Voc.	ἀληθές	ἀληθές	ἀληθεῖς	ἀληθῆ
Acc.	ἀληθῆ	ἀληθές	ἀληθεῖς	ἀληθῆ
Gen.	ἀληθοῦς	ἀληθοῦς	ἀληθῶν	ἀληθῶν
Dat.	ἀληθεῖ	ἀληθεῖ	ἀληθέσι(ν)	ἀληθέσι(ν)

§3 ADJECTIVAL AGREEMENT

An adjective agrees with its noun in gender, number and case.

καλὸς λίθος or λίθος καλός *a beautiful stone*
λίθοις καλοῖς (Lk.21:5)
μέλι ἄγριον (Mk 1:6)
ἐν πνεύματι ἁγίῳ (Mk 1:8)
ἐν πνεύματι ἀκαθάρτῳ (Mk 1:23)
ἀγέλη χοίρων μεγάλη (Mk 5:11)
ἀνὴρ ἀγαθός (Acts 11:24)

§4 INDEFINITE ADJECTIVE

An indefinite adjective can stand on its own without a definite article, with or without a noun.

'Ιωσὴφ δίκαιος ὤν (Mt.1:19)
καλὸς κἀγαθός *handsome and good* (i.e., *a gentleman* in classical Greek)[1]

ἦν ἀνὴρ ἀγαθὸς καὶ πλήρης πνεύματος ἁγίου καὶ πίστεως. (Acts 11:24)

§5 ATTRIBUTIVE ADJECTIVES

When the adjectival phrase contains the definite article, the adjective must be immediately preceded by the definite article if being used attributively, i.e., attributing some quality to the noun. This means that an adjective in attributive position is preceded by the definite article. Thus: ὁ ἀγαθὸς δοῦλος or ὁ δοῦλος ὁ ἀγαθός = *the good slave*.

ὁ υἱός μου ὁ ἀγαπητός   (Mk 1:11)
ἔθυσας αὐτῷ τὸν σιτευτὸν μόσχον   (Lk.15:30)

§6 PREDICATIVE ADJECTIVES

When the adjective is being used predicatively, i.e., as part of the predicate or verb, it is not immediately preceded by the definite article. (Cf. use of noun without article in Jn 1:1 – θεὸς ἦν ὁ λόγος.) If no verb is expressed, part of the verb "to be" can be understood. Thus: ὁ δοῦλος ἀγαθός or ἀγαθὸς ὁ δοῦλος = *the slave is good*.

μακάριοι οἱ πτωχοὶ τῷ πνεύματι. (Mt.5:3)

ἡ ἐντολὴ ἁγία καὶ δικαία καὶ ἀγαθή. (Rom.7:12)

---

[1] For **crasis**, see 1§27.

§7 ADJECTIVES AS NOUNS

An adjective can be converted into a noun by prefixing the definite article:

οἱ ἅγιοι = *the holy ones, saints*

ἡ ἔρημος (χώρα) = *the deserted* (place), *desert, wilderness*

ἐν τῇ ἐρήμῳ = *in the desert* (Mk 1:4)

§8 ATTRIBUTIVE ADJECTIVES IN PREDICATIVE POSITION

(1) Certain adjectives or pronouns used as adjectives are always in predicative position even when used attributively.

οὗτος	αὕτη	τοῦτο	= *this*
ἐκεῖνος	ἐκείνη	ἐκεῖνο	= *that*
ὅλος	ὅλη	ὅλον	= *whole*

ἐν ἐκείνῃ τῇ ἡμέρᾳ	(Mk 4:35)
ἐν ἐκείναις ταῖς ἡμέραις	(Mk 1:9)
ὅλη ἡ πόλις	(Mk 1:33)
εἰς ὅλην τὴν Γαλιλαίαν	(Mk 1:39)

(2) The **Demonstrative Adjective/Pronoun** οὗτος (= *this, these)* is declined as follows:

| | **Singular** | | | **Plural** | | |
	Masc.	**Fem.**	**Neut.**	**Masc.**	**Fem.**	**Neut.**
Nom.	οὗτος	αὕτη	τοῦτο	οὗτοι	αὗται	ταῦτα
Acc.	τοῦτον	ταύτην	τοῦτο	τούτους	ταύτας	ταῦτα
Gen.	τούτου	ταύτης	τούτου	τούτων	τούτων	τούτων
Dat.	τούτῳ	ταύτῃ	τούτῳ	τούτοις	ταύταις	τούτοις

(3) When used as a demonstrative adjective, it must be in predicative position.

(4)   It should be noted that the genitive plural is the same for all genders.

(5)   Wherever there is an o/ω in the ending, the first syllable has ου not αυ.

(6)   The **Demonstrative Adjective/Pronoun** ἐκεῖνος (= *that, those*) is declined as follows:

| | Singular | | | Plural | | |
	Masc.	**Fem.**	**Neut.**	**Masc.**	**Fem.**	**Neut.**
Nom.	ἐκεῖνος	ἐκείνη	ἐκεῖνο	ἐκεῖνοι	ἐκεῖναι	ἐκεῖνα
Acc.	ἐκεῖνον	ἐκείνην	ἐκεῖνο	ἐκείνους	ἐκείνας	ἐκεῖνα
Gen.	ἐκείνου	ἐκείνης	ἐκείνου	ἐκείνων	ἐκείνων	ἐκείνων
Dat.	ἐκείνῳ	ἐκείνῃ	ἐκείνῳ	ἐκείνοις	ἐκείναις	ἐκείνοις

(7)   As a demonstrative adjective, it is always found in predicative position, like οὗτος.

ἡ βασιλεία ἐκείνη = *that kingdom* (Mk 3:24)

ἡ οἰκία ἐκείνη = *that house* (Mk 3:25)

ἐκείνοις τοῖς ἔξω = *to those outside* (Mk 4:11)

§9   ALL, EVERY, WHOLE

(1)   πᾶς πᾶσα πᾶν can also be used in predicative position. It means **all, every, whole**.

(2)   It is declined as follows:

	SINGULAR		
Nom.	πᾶς	πᾶσα	πᾶν
Acc.	πάντα	πᾶσαν	πᾶν
Gen.	παντός	πάσης	παντός
Dat.	παντί	πάσῃ	παντί
	PLURAL		
Nom.	πάντες	πᾶσαι	πάντα
Acc.	πάντας	πάσας	πάντα
Gen.	πάντων	πασῶν	πάντων
Dat.	πᾶσι(ν)	πάσαις	πᾶσι(ν)

(3)   When it occurs with an indefinite noun in the singular it means "every". In the plural, it means "all". Used with the article (either before or after it), it can mean "whole".

πᾶν δένδρον = *every tree* (Mt.7:17)

οἱ Ἱεροσολυμῖται πάντες = *all the people of Jerusalem* (Mk 1:5)

πᾶσα ἡ Ἰουδαία χώρα = *the whole Judaean countryside* (Mk 1:5)

§10   He/she/it – SAME/SELF

(1)   αὐτός αὐτή αὐτό can be used as **3rd person personal pronouns** meaning *he/she/it*.

(2)   They are declined as follows:

| | **Singular** | | | **Plural** | | |
	Masc.	**Fem.**	**Neut.**	**Masc.**	**Fem.**	**Neut.**
Nom.	αὐτός	αὐτή	αὐτό	αὐτοί	αὐταί	αὐτά
Acc.	αὐτόν	αὐτήν	αὐτό	αὐτούς	αὐτάς	αὐτά
Gen.	αὐτοῦ	αὐτῆς	αὐτοῦ	αὐτῶν	αὐτῶν	αὐτῶν
Dat.	αὐτῷ	αὐτῇ	αὐτῷ	αὐτοῖς	αὐταῖς	αὐτοῖς

(3)   The following are examples of this as a personal pronoun in Mark:

τὸ πνεῦμα αὐτὸν ἐκβάλλει εἰς τὴν ἔρημον. (Mk 1:12)
The Spirit drives him out (historic present) *into the desert.*

καὶ ἀφῆκεν αὐτὴν ὁ πυρετός, καὶ διηκόνει αὐτοῖς. (Mk 1:31)
And the fever left her and she was waiting upon them.

(4)   As adjectives, they are found either in attributive position = *same* or in predicative position = *self*.

ὁ αὐτὸς πατήρ or ὁ πατὴρ ὁ αὐτός = *the same father*

αὐτὸς γὰρ ὁ πατὴρ φιλεῖ ὑμεῖς (Jn 16:27)
For the Father himself loves you.

δεῦτε ὑμεῖς αὐτοὶ κατ' ἰδίαν εἰς ἔρημον τόπον (Mk 6:31)
Come you yourselves privately into a desert place.

§11 PERSONAL PRONOUNS

The first and second persons of the personal pronoun – *I/we*; *you* – are declined as follows:

Singular	Nom.	ἐγώ	σύ
	Acc.	ἐμέ, με	σέ, σε
	Gen.	ἐμοῦ, μου	σοῦ, σου
	Dat.	ἐμοῖ, μοι	σοῖ, σοι
Plural	Nom.	ἡμεῖς	ὑμεῖς
	Acc.	ἡμᾶς	ὑμᾶς
	Gen.	ἡμῶν	ὑμῶν
	Dat.	ἡμῖν	ὑμῖν

§12 ADVERBS OF MANNER

Adverbs of manner, i.e., answering the question πῶς; = how? are formed from adjectives by changing the last syllable of the genitive singular masculine into -ως; but note οὕτως without τ-.

τί οὗτος οὕτως λαλεῖ; = *Why is this man speaking thus?*
(Mk 2:7)

καλως πάντα πεποίηκεν = *He has done all things well.*
(Mk 7:37)

§13 COMPARISON OF ADJECTIVES

(1) The most usual way to form comparatives and superlatives is to add -οτερος and -οτατος to the stem. When the preceding syllable is short this is lengthened to -ωτερος and -ωτατος.

σοφός	σοφώτερος	σοφώτατος	(*wise, wiser, wisest*)
δίκαιος	δικαιότερος	δικαιότατος	(*righteous, more righteous, most righteous*)
ἰσχυρός	ἰσχυρότερος	ἰσχυρότατος	(*strong, -er, -est*)

τί ἐστιν εὐκοπώτερον; (Mk 2:9)

(2)   Notice the following irregular comparisons:

ἀγαθός   κρείσσων   κράτιστος   (*good, better, best*)
                                   (κράτιστε Θεόφιλε – Lk.1:3)

κακός   χείρων   (χεῖρον σχίσμα γίνεται – Mk 2:21)
(bad, worse)   (μᾶλλον εἰς τὸ χεῖρον ἐλθοῦσα – Mk 5:26)

μέγας   μείζων   μέγιστος   (*great, greater,
                                   greatest*)

μικρός   μικρότερος ἐλάχιστος   (*small, smaller,
                                   smallest*)

πολύς   πλείων   (*much, more*)

(3)   Comparative adjectives and adverbs can be followed either by the genitive case or by ἤ = *than* with the same case.

ἔρχεται ὁ ἰσχυρότερός μου ὀπίσω μου. (Mk 1:7)
The stronger than I is coming after me.

μικρότερον ὂν πάντων τῶν σπερμάτων τῶν ἐπὶ τῆς γῆς
(4:31)
being smaller (= smallest) of all the seeds upon the earth

μείζων τούτων ἄλλη ἐντολὴ οὐκ ἔστιν. (Mk 12:31)
There is not another commandment greater than these.

ἠγάπησαν οἱ ἄνθρωποι μᾶλλον τὸ σκότος ἤ τὸ φῶς.
(Jn 3:19)
The people loved the darkness more than the light.

(4)   A comparative adjective is sometimes found instead of a superlative, which is less frequent in the New Testament. See Mk 4:31 quoted in (3).

ὁ δὲ μικρότερος ἐν τῇ βασιλείᾳ τοῦ θεοῦ μείζων αὐτοῦ ἐστιν.
(Lk.7:28)

§14   ADJECTIVAL CLAUSES

(1)   In English, an adjectival clause is introduced by a relative pronoun – "who", "whom", "whose", "which", "that"; e.g.,

The man/the woman *who is speaking* is famous; The people *to whom they are speaking* are listening; The author *whose book we are reading* is wise; Things *which/that grow* are beautiful. Notice that the relative pronoun changes depending on whether we are describing things or persons and also on whether the pronoun stands for the subject or object or indirect object of its own clause.

(2) Similarly, in Greek there are relative pronouns which function in the same kind of way. The rule is that a relative pronoun agrees with its antecedent (i.e., the noun or pronoun to which it refers in the main clause) in gender, number, but *not usually* in case. Its case depends on its function within its own clause. If it is the subject, then it is in the nominative case. If it is the object, then it is in the accusative case. If it is the indirect object, then it is in the dative case. If it involves possession (= *whose*), then it is in the genitive case.

(3) The paradigm is as follows:

	Masculine	*Feminine*	*Neuter*
	SINGULAR		
Nom.	ὅς	ἥ	ὅ
Acc.	ὅν	ἥν	ὅ
Gen.	οὗ	ἧς	οὗ
Dat.	ᾧ	ᾗ	ᾧ
	PLURAL		
Nom.	οἵ	αἵ	ἅ
Acc.	οὕς	ἅς	ἅ
Gen.	ὧν	ὧν	ὧν
Dat.	οἷς	αἷς	οἷς

(4) Notice carefully how this differs from the definite article. Unlike the article, it always begins with a rough breathing. Where the article begins with a rough breathing – ὁ ἡ οἱ αἱ – it does not have an accent, while the relative pronoun always has either an acute accent (which becomes grave before another word) or a circumflex accent.

(5)   For examples of the relative pronoun in Mark, see

1:2 – ὃς κατασκευάσει
1:7 – οὗ οὐκ εἰμὶ ἱκανὸς λῦσαι τὸν ἱμάντα τῶν ὑποδημάτων
αὐτοῦ
2:19 – ἐν ᾧ (= *while*)

(6)   Occasionally, the relative pronoun is attracted into the case of its antecedent, as in Mk 7:13.

. . . τῇ παραδόσει ὑμῶν ᾗ (not ἣν) παρεδώκατε.
. . . *by your tradition which you handed on.*

§15   NUMERALS

(1)   The numeral *one* is declined as follows:

	Masculine	Feminine	Neuter
Nom.	εἷς	μία	ἕν
Acc.	ἕνα	μίαν	ἕν
Gen.	ἑνός	μιᾶς	ἑνός
Dat.	ἑνί	μιᾷ	ἑνί

(2)   δύο with dative δυσί(ν) = *two*

(3)   τρεῖς (masc./fem.), τρία (neut.) = *three*

(4)   τέτταρες (masc./fem.), τέτταρα (neut.) = *four*

(5)   πέντε = *five.*

ASSIGNMENTS

1.   Translate all the Greek phrases and sentences used as examples in this lesson and check your translation by referring to a modern English version of the New Testament.

2. **LEARN BY HEART** the present indicative active of the
Greek verb εἶναι = to be:

Singular:	1st person	εἰμί	I am
	2nd person	εἶ	you are
	3rd person	ἐστί(ν)	he/she/it is
Plural:	1st person	ἐσμέν	we are
	2nd person	ἐστέ	you are
	3rd person	εἰσί(ν)	they are

3. **REMEMBER** that the verb "to be" takes a **complement**
not an object. This means that, both in English and in Greek,
it takes the same case after it as before it.

> The father is wise. ὁ πατήρ ἐστι σοφός
> or   σοφός ἐστιν ὁ πατήρ.[2]

4. In such a clause in Greek, the verb can even be left out.

> σοφὸς ὁ πατήρ. [See §4 above.]

5. Note that ἦν is both the 1st person singular and the 3rd
person singular of the imperfect indicative active of εἶναι (=
to be). So it can mean either *I was/used to be* or *he/she/it was/
used to be*.

6. Write down and learn the following Greek adjectives:

	Meaning
ἀγαθός, -ή, -όν	good
ἅγιος, -α, -ον	holy
δίκαιος, -α, -ον	righteous
ἰσχυρός, -α, -ον	strong
καινός, -ή, -όν	new
κακός, -ή, -όν	bad
καλός, -ή, -όν	beautiful
μακάριος, -α, -ον	happy, blessed
μέγας, μεγάλη, μέγα	large
μικρός, -ά, -όν	small
πολύς, πολλή, πολύ	much, many
σοφός, -ή, -όν	wise

[2] All forms of the present indicative active of the verb εἶναι are enclitic
[see 3§6(5)], except the 2nd personal singular - εἶ. This means that, if
possible, they throw the accent back on to the previous word [see 'Εγώ εἰμι
in 1§3]. The accent remains acute.

7.   Translate into English:

(1)   Σὺ εἶ ὁ Χριστός. (Mk 8:29)

(2)   Σὺ εἶ υἱὸς τοῦ Θεοῦ. (Mk 3:11)

(3)   Σὺ εἶ ὁ υἱός μου ὁ ἀγαπητός. (Mk 1:11)

8.   Translate into Greek:

   (1)   This prophet is good.
   (2)   I am the son of my father.
   (3)   That messenger is speaking about the good news.
   (4)   Blessed is the whole city.
   (5)   The father himself loves you.
   (6)   The same lord is announcing the beginning of the gospel.
   (7)   Joseph was a just man.

9.   Identify the relative pronoun in Mk 2:24. How do you know this is *not* the definite article?

10.   Identify the relative pronoun in Mk 2:26 and its antecedent.

11.   Identify the relative pronoun in Mk 3:13. The antecedent has to be supplied. It would be something like ἐκείνους = *those men.*

12.   Ὅς ἔχει ὦτα ἀκούειν ἀκουέτω. (Mk 4:9) What antecedent would you supply here? Can you translate the whole sentence into English?

13.   Explain the difference between οἱ and οἵ in Mk 4:16?[3]

14.   Mk 6 contains several numerals. Note the genitive in 6:3 – ἄρτους δηναρίων διακοσίων – *loaves worth 200 denarii.*[4] So διακόσιοι, -αι, – α = 200. Notice also δώδεκα = *12* (6:7), πεντήκοντα = *50* (6:40), ἑκατόν = *100* (6:40), πεντακισχίλιοι = *5000* (6:44).

[3] See 4§14(4).

[4] See 3§14.

(1)   If πέντε = 5 and -κισ- = *times*, what does χίλιοι mean?

(2)   Translate πεντακισχίλιοι ἄνδρες.[5]

(3)   How many people did Jesus feed with the five loaves and the two fish? See Mt.14:21 – χωρὶς γυναικῶν καὶ παιδίων.

---

[5] See 3§12(8).

CHAPTER FIVE

Verb Stems

§1 PRINCIPAL PARTS

(1) When one is asked to give the principal parts of a Greek verb, one has to provide the 1st person singular of six tenses, where they exist:

Present	Indicative Active
Future	Indicative Active
Aorist	Indicative Active
Perfect	Indicative Active
Perfect	Indicative Middle/Passive
Aorist	Indicative Passive

(2) Not all verbs have all six.

(3) The principal parts of λύω are:

λύω λύσω ἔλυσα λέλυκα λέλυμαι ἐλύθην *I loose*

(4) From these principal parts one can form all the other tenses of the Greek verb.

(5) Some Greek verbs have only one stem, from which all the principal parts and all the tenses are formed. The stem of λύω is λυ-. From this stem all tenses are formed.

§2   VERBS WITH TWO STEMS

(1)   Many Greek verbs have two stems – verbal and present.

+++

VERBAL STEM → **Future Active**   **Future Passive**
                  (and Middle)

                  Aorist Active   **Aorist Passive**
                  (and Middle)

                  Perfect Active → **Perfect Middle/Passive**
                  (and Pluperfect
                  Active)

                              (and Pluperfect Middle/Passive)

PRESENT STEM → **Present Active** (and Middle/Passive)
                  (and Imperfect Active/Middle/Passive)

+++

(2)   Even though the present stem is the one found in dictionaries in the form of the 1st person singular of the present indicative active, **the verbal stem** is the more important.

(3)   The present stem is often formed from the verbal stem by lengthening or some other process.

(4)   From the verbal stem, one can form not only the present stem but also all the tenses except present and imperfect – future, aorist, perfect, pluperfect – in all voices and moods.

§3   THE PRESENT STEM

(1)   The present stem can be formed from the verbal stem by lengthening.

(2)   In certain cases, especially where the verbal stem ends in
-π, the present stem is formed by adding τ; e.g., from the
verbal stem καλυπ- the present stem is καλυπτ-.

καλύπτω καλύψω ἐκάλυψα κεκάλυφα κεκάλυμμαι ἐκαλύφθην
I hide[1]

(3)   From this verb, there comes a compound verb with the
preposition ἀπό (= *away*) prefixed – ἀποκαλύπτω = I reveal.
The cognate noun[2] – ἡ ἀποκάλυψις = revelation – gives us *the
Apocalypse* in English – *the Book of Revelation.*[3]

(4)   From the stem κρυπ- we get

κρύπτω κρύψω ἔκρυψα κέκρυφα κέκρυμμαι ἐκρύφθην *I hide*

(5)   In Mk 1:7, we find the nominative singular masculine of
the aorist participle from the verb κύπτω = *I bend down* –
κύψας = *having bent down.*

§4   GUTTURAL ENDING

(1)   When the verbal stem ends in a guttural – e.g., γ or κ –
this can be softened to σσ to form the present tense.

(2)   The Greek word for *herald* is ὁ κῆρυξ and the word for
proclamation or *preaching* is τὸ κήρυγμα. The cognate verb is
κηρύσσω. All these words come from the same root κηρυκ-. The
verbal stem is also κηρυκ-. So

κηρύσσω κηρύξω ἐκήρυξα κεκήρυχα κεκήρυγμαι ἐκηρύχθην
I preach

---

[1] In Homer, ἡ Καλυψώ was a nymph, the daughter of Atlas, so-called because
she hid Ulysses on his return from Troy.

[2] A cognate noun is one formed from the same root as the verb.

[3] This is one of many examples of apocalyptic literature. Compare also the
little apocalypse in Mark 13 and the Book of Daniel.

(3)   From the root πραγ we get the English word pragmatics and also one of the Greek verbs meaning "I do".

πράσσω πράξω ἔπραξα πέπραχα πέπραγμαι ἐπράχθην *I do*

(4)   Cf. τὸ πρᾶγμα = *deed, occurrence, event.*

§5   DENTAL ENDING

(1)   When the verbal stem ends in a dental – e.g., δ – this can fall out before σ in the formation of the future and the aorist and lengthens to -ζω for the present stem.

(2)   Thus,

βαπτίζω βαπτίσω ἐβάπτισα ——— βεβάπτισμαι ἐβαπτίσθην
I dip, baptize

(3)   So John was called ὁ βαπτίζων (**present participle**) = *the baptizing one*, because he actually dipped or immersed people into the water; hence, ὁ Βαπτιστής used as a surname.

(4)   Compare

δοξάζω δοξάσω ἐδόξασα ——— δεδόξασμαι ἐδοξάσθην
I glorify

(5)   This is found especially in John's Gospel – see, e.g., Jn 7:39; 8:54; 11:4; 17:10.

§6   ΚΡΑΖΩ

(1)   Special care should be taken with κράζω. Note that the stem ends in a guttural: κραγ-. So it takes its future in ξ.

κράζω κράξω ἔκραξα κέκραγα ——— ———
I cry out

(2)   See, e.g., Mk 3:11; 5:5, 7; Jn 1:15; 7:28.

§7 ΛΛ from Λ

(1) Other forms of lengthening of present stem occur. For example, λλ from λ.

> βάλλω βαλῶ ἔβαλον⁴ βέβληκα βέβλημαι ἐβλήθην
> *I throw*

(2) Compare

> στέλλω στελῶ ἔστειλα ἔσταλκα ἔσταλμαι ἐστάλην
> *I send*

This is usually found in the compound form ἀποστέλλω = *I send out*. The cognate noun is ἀπόστολος. So *an apostle* is someone who has been sent out.

§8 -ΣΚ-

(1) A few verbs lengthen with -σκ-.

> εὑρίσκω εὑρήσω εὗρον εὕρηκα εὕρημαι εὑρέθην
> *I find*

(2) Compare

> διδάσκω διδάξω ἐδίδαξα ——— ——— ἐδιδάχθην
> *I teach*

§9 DEFECTIVE VERBS

In addition to these verbs which form their present stem by lengthening the verbal stem, there are a few defective Greek verbs found in the New Testament which draw on parts from other Greek roots to help them form some principal parts.

---

⁴ See 5§10.

(1) ἔρχομαι ἐλεύσομαι ἦλθον ἐλήλυθα ———— *I come, go*

(2) ἐσθίω φάγομαι ἔφαγον ——— ——— ——— *I eat*

(3) λέγω ἐρῶ εἶπον εἴρηκα ——— ——— *I speak, say*

(4) ὁράω ὄψομαι εἶδον ἑώρακα/ἑόρακα —— ὤφθην *I see*

(5) τρέχω δραμοῦμαι ἔδραμον δεδράμηκα δεδράμημαι — *I run*

(6) φέρω οἴσω ἤνεγκον/ἤνεγκα ἐνήνοχα ἐνήνεγμαι ἠνέχθην *I carry*

§10 SECOND or STRONG AORIST

(1) Many Greek verbs have a strong or second aorist form in addition to or, more often, instead of the first or weak aorist.

(2) The first aorist is formed from the verbal stem by adding σ before the endings: augment + stem + σ + endings – thus,

$$ἔ – λυ – σ – α.$$

(3) The second aorist is formed by adding the endings of the imperfect tense to the verbal stem rather than to the present stem, as for the imperfect tense: augment + verbal stem + imperfect endings – thus, ἔ – βαλ – ον. Cf. imperfect – ἔβαλλον.

(4) The second aorist infinitive has the same ending as the present infinitive but is added to the verbal stem, not the present stem.

Aorist Infinitive – βαλεῖν

Present Infinitive – βάλλειν.

(5) Similarly, the endings for the second aorist imperatives are the same as for the present imperatives, but they are added to the verbal stem, not the present stem, as in the case of the present imperatives.

Aorist Imperatives – βάλε βαλέτω βάλετε βαλέτωσαν

Present Imperatives – βάλλε βαλλέτω βάλλετε βαλλέτωσαν

(6) The endings of second aorist participles are the same as for present participles, but they are added to the verbal stem rather than to the present stem. Notice also the different accentuation:

Present	βάλλων	βάλλουσα	βᾶλλον
Aorist	βαλών	βαλοῦσα	βαλόν

§11 PARSING

(1) It is important from an early stage in learning Greek to parse every word in a sentence. This should be done automatically before translating into English.

(2) In parsing **a noun**, one is expected to indicate case, number, nominative singular with definite article (indicating gender) and meaning. Thus,

εὐαγγελίου: genitive singular of τὸ εὐαγγέλιον = *good news, gospel*

(3) In parsing a verb, one should give person, number, tense, mood, voice, 1st person singular of the present indicative , and meaning.

λύεις

2nd person singular of present indicative active of λύω *I loose.*

ASSIGNMENTS

1. **PARSE** the following verbs from Mark 1:1–11

    (1) κατασκευάσει (Mk 1:2) – see 2A4(2)n18

    (2) ἐκήρυσσεν (Mk 1:7) – see 2A4(3)

    (3) ἐβάπτισα (Mk 1:8) – see 2A4(1)

(4) βαπτίσει (Mk 1:8) – see 2A4(2)
(5) εἶ (Mk 1:11) – see 4A2
(6) εὐδόκησα (Mk 1:11) – see 2§10(4)

2. **SEE Appendix 2: Principal Parts of Common Greek Verbs.**
WRITE DOWN and LEARN the principal parts of ἀγγέλλω,
ἀκούω, ἀποθνῄσκω[5] and ἀποκτείνω.

3. If λύει is 3rd person singular of the present indicative active
of λύω = *I loose*, how would you parse παραγγέλλει (Mk 8:6)?

4. PARSE (1) ἀκούουσιν (Mk 4:20) [Cf. λύουσιν - 2§8(3)]

(2) ἤκουσεν (Mk 6:14) [Cf. ἔλυσεν – 2§18(10)]

5. PARSE (1) τέθνηκεν (Mk 15:44) [Cf. λέλυκεν – 2§8(12)]

(2) ἐκήρυσσεν (Mk 1:7) [Cf. ἔλυεν – 2§8(7)]

(3) ἐκήρυξαν (Mk 6:12) [Cf. ἔλυσαν – 2§8(10)]

(4) ἐκήρυσσον (Mk 7:36) [Cf. ἔλυον - 2§8(7)]

6. **TRANSLATE into English:**

(1) ἀποστέλλω τὸν ἄγγελόν μου πρὸ προσώπου σου. (Mk 1:2)

(2) τί ἀκούετε; (Cf. Mk 4:24)

(3) ἡ θυγάτηρ σου ἀπέθανεν. (Mk 5:35)

(4) ἤθελεν αὐτὸν ἀποκτεῖναι. (Mk 6:19)

7. **TRANSLATE into Greek:**

(1) Have you (singular) heard (perfect) the good news of God?
(2) I shall preach to the people. [See 3§3(7)]
(3) Do you (singular) have ears to hear? (Cf. Mk 4:23)
(4) The prophet is writing. (Cf. Mk 1:2)

---

[5] ἀποθνῄσκω ἀποθανοῦμαι (fut.) ἀπέθανον (aor.) τέθνηκα (perf.)

CHAPTER SIX

The Greek Verb: Voice

§1 TWO ENGLISH VOICES[1]

§1   In English, the verb has two voices – **active and passive**. The active voice indicates that the subject of the sentence is actively doing something or other. In the passive voice, the subject of the sentence is being acted upon. Thus, *Bill is hitting a ball* (active); *A ball is being hit by Bill* (passive).

§2   THREE GREEK VOICES

(1)   In Greek, there are **three voices** – active, middle and passive.

(2)   The Greek active and passive correspond to the English active and passive.

> **Active:** ὁ ᾽Ιωάννης βαπτίζει τὸν ᾽Ιησοῦν.
> *John is baptizing Jesus.*

> **Passive:** ὁ ᾽Ιησοῦς βαπτίζεται ὑπὸ τοῦ ᾽Ιωάννου.
> *Jesus is being baptized by John.*

(3)   Note that the passive voice is usually followed by ὑπό with the genitive of the agent. The instrument can be expressed by ἐν with the dative or by the simple dative.

> ὁ ἀπόστολος λύεται ὑπὸ τοῦ ἀγγέλου λόγῳ.
> *The apostle is being loosed by the messenger with a word.*

---

[1] See 2§3.

§3   THE MIDDLE VOICE

(1)   The **middle voice** in Greek is sometimes reflexive, like the
reflexive verb in French; e.g., je me couche = *I am going to
bed*; je me lave = *I am washing myself.*

Active: λούω τὸ βρέφος.
I am washing the baby.

Passive: τὸ βρέφος λούεται ὑπό μου.
The baby is being washed by me.

Middle: λούομαι.
I am washing myself.

Active: ἐνδύω τὸ ἱμάτιον τὸ τέκνον.
I am clothing the child with a garment.
[Note the double accusative after a verb of *clothing.*]

Middle: ἐνδύομαι τὸ ἱμάτιον.
I am putting the garment on myself.

Passive: ἐνδύομαι ὑπὸ τοῦ δούλου.
I am being clothed by the slave.
[Note that the middle and passive are exactly the same in form.]

(2)   However, it is probably truer to say that the middle voice
in Greek primarily signifies not reflexive action but action that
is of advantage to the subject or that is done for the subject.
So λύεται is not primarily *he is loosing himself* but *he is loosing
for himself.*[2]

(3)   Compare Jn 13:14 with Mt.27:24.

Active: ἐγω ἔνιψα ὑμῶν τοὺς πόδας. (Jn 13:14)
I washed your feet.

---

[2] Cf. French **se brosser** = *to brush oneself*; but **il se brosse les dents** = *he is
brushing his teeth.* Cf. **Je me lave les mains** = *I am washing my hands.*

Middle: ὁ Πιλᾶτος . . . λαβὼν ὕδωρ ἀπενίψατο τὰς χεῖρας
ἀπέναντι τοῦ ὄχλου. (Mt.27:24)
*Pilate, having taken water, washed [his] hands in front of the
people.*

(4)   See Mk 6:9 – μὴ ἐνδύσησθε δύο ζιτῶνας = *Do not put
on two tunics.*

(5)   More often, the reflexive element in the Greek middle
voice is conspicuous by its absence. It is very close to being
active in meaning.

(6)   By the time of Hellenistic Greek, the middle was falling
out of use. It is not always found in the New Testament where
one might expect it. Compare Mk 10:20, where we find the
middle –

ταῦτα πάντα ἐφυλαξάμην ἐκ νεότητός μου.
I kept all these from my youth.

– with Mt.19:20 and Lk.18:21, where the active voice is found
– ἐφύλαξα.[3]

§4   DEPONENT VERBS

(1)   Many middle verbs have no active form. They are active
in meaning though middle (or passive) in form. Such verbs are
called **deponent verbs** – that is, they have **placed aside** – from
Latin ponere = *to place* and de- = *down* or *aside* – their active
forms.

(2)   A deponent verb, therefore, is a verb which is middle or
passive in form but active in meaning.

(3)   Examples of deponent verbs found in the New Testament
are:

---

[3] It may seem odd to have the aorist tense here. It has been described as an
ingressive or inceptive aorist indicating the point of entrance into the state.
The man may be expressing not so much a boast as dissatisfaction with
himself and perhaps even with the reply given by Jesus to his question.

ἀποκρίνομαι = I answer; cf. active κρίνω = I judge
          aorist (passive in form): ἀπεκρίθην
ἅπτομαι = I touch (takes genitive case)
ἀρνέομαι > ἀρνοῦμαι = I deny
βούλομαι = I wish
γίνομαι = I become; future – γενήσομαι; aorist middle –
ἐγενόμην; aorist passive – ἐγενήθην
δέχομαι = I receive
ἔρχομαι = I come/go – future: ἐλεύσομαι (see Mk 2:20)
πορεύομαι = I go on a journey (see compound verbs in Mk
                                              1:21; 2:23)
φοβέομαι φοβοῦμαι = I am afraid;
     see Mk 16:8 – ἐφοβοῦντο γάρ; cf. ὁ φόβος = fear/awe.

§5   VERBS WITH MIDDLE FUTURE

(1)   Some verbs that are active in the present take a middle
form in the future.

(2)   ὁράω (= *I see*); ὄψομαι (= *I shall see*). The root οπ
occurs again in the aorist passive, which is ὤφθην. This
comes into English in such words as *optics* and *optician*.

(3)   γινώσκω (= *I know*); γνώσομαι (= *I shall know*).

(4)   λαμβάνω (= *I take, receive*); λήψομαι or λήμψομαι (= *I
shall take, receive)*. This is often found in the compound form
παραλαμβάνω = *I receive, accept tradition*.

§6   CHANGE OF MEANING IN MIDDLE

(1)   A few verbs change their meaning when they move from
the active voice into the middle. Thus,

(2)   ἄρχω (= I *rule*); ἄρχομαι (= *I begin*). The cognate
noun is ἡ ἀρχή (= *the beginning* or *rule*). See Mk 1:1 for its
use in the sense of *beginning* without the definite article,
presumably because it is a heading to the whole gospel or to
the prologue.

(3) ἅπτω (= *I light, ignite*); ἅπτομαι (= *I touch*).

ὁ 'Ιησοῦς ἥψατο αὐτοῦ. (Mk 1:21)
Jesus touched him.
[Note that this verb takes the genitive of the person or thing
touched.]

καὶ ὅσοι ἂν ἥψαντο αὐτοῦ ἐσώζοντο. (Mk 6:56)
And those who touched him were being saved.

§7 MIDDLE AND PASSIVE FORMS

(1) Middle and passive have the same forms in four tenses –
present, imperfect, perfect and pluperfect. They have separate
forms for future and aorist. See Appendix 1: *The Regular
Greek Verb.*

(2) Present Middle and Passive:

Person	Singular	Plural
1st	λύ-ομαι	λυ-όμεθα
2nd	λύ-ῃ	λύ-εσθε
3rd	λύ-εται	λύ-ονται

(3) Imperfect Middle and Passive:

Person	Singular	Plural
1st	ἐ-λυ-όμην	ἐ-λυ-όμεθα
2nd	ἐ-λύ-ου	ἐ-λύ-εσθε
3rd	ἐ-λύ-ετc	ἐ-λύ-οντο

(4) Perfect Middle and Passive:

Person	Singular	Plural
1st	λέ-λυ-μαι	λε-λύ-μεθα
2nd	λέ-λυ-σαι	λέ-λυ-σθε
3rd	λέ-λυ-ται	λέ-λυ-νται.

(5) Pluperfect Middle and Passive

Person	Singular	Plural
1st	(ἐ)-λε-λύ-μην	(ἐ)-λε-λύ-μεθα
2nd	(ἐ)-λέ-λύ-σο	(ἐ)-λέ-λυ-σθε
3rd	(ἐ)-λέ-λυ-το	(ἐ)-λέ-λυ-ντο

§8 FUTURE AND AORIST MIDDLE

(1) The future middle has σ inserted between the stem and the endings for the present middle.

Person	Singular	Plural
1st	λύ-σ-ομαι	λυ-σ-όμεθα
2nd	λύ-σ-η	λύ-σ-εσθε
3rd	λύ-σ-εται	λύ-σ-ονται

(2) The aorist middle has σ inserted between the stem and the endings of the aorist middle.

Person	Singular	Plural
1st	ἐ-λυ-σ-άμην	ἐ-λυ-σ-άμεθα
2nd	ἐ-λύ-σ-ω	ἐ-λύ-σ-ασθε
3rd	ἐ-λύ-σ-ατο	ἐ-λύ-σ-αντο

§9 FUTURE AND AORIST PASSIVE

(1) The future passive is characterized by the insertion of θησ between the stem and the same endings as for the present middle and passive and for the future middle.

Person	Singular	Plural
1st	λυ-θήσ-ομαι	λυ-θησ-όμεθα
2nd	λυ-θήσ-η	λυ-θήσ-εσθε
3rd	λυ-θήσ-εται	λυ-θήσ-ονται

(2) The aorist indicative passive has the augment plus the stem plus θ plus the aorist passive endings.

Person	Singular	Plural
1st	ἐ-λύ-θην	ἐ-λύ-θημεν
2nd	ἐ-λύ-θης	ἐ-λύ-θητε
3rd	ἐ-λύ-θη	ἐ-λύ-θησαν

ASSIGNMENTS

1. See Appendix 2. **WRITE DOWN and LEARN the principal parts** of βαίνω, βάλλω, γίνομαι, γινώσκω and γράφω.

2. **LEARN** the aorist indicative active of βαίνω: ἔβην, ἔβης, ἔβη, ἔβημεν, ἔβητε, ἔβησαν. The aorist infinitive is βῆναι.

3. **PARSE** ἐμβῆναι (Mk 6:45), ἀνέβη (Mk 6:51), κατέβη (Lk.2:51). **NOTE** that βαίνω is never found as a simple verb in the New Testament but always as a compound with prepositions.

4. **SEE** 5§10 for the strong aorist of βάλλω. **PARSE** ἐκβάλλει (Mk 1:12), βάλλει (Mk 2:22), βαλεῖν (Mk 7:27), ἔβαλεν (Mk 7:33).

5. **PARSE** ἐγένετο (Mk 1:4), γίνεται (Mk 2:15), γέγονεν (Mk 5:33).

6. **LEARN** the aorist indicative active of γινώσκω: ἔγνων, ἔγνως, ἔγνω, ἔγνωμεν, ἔγνωτε, ἔγνωσαν. The infinitive is γνῶναι. **PARSE** ἔγνω (Mk 5:29), ἐπέγνωσαν (Mk 6:33).

7. **NOTE** the compound verb ἀναγινώσκω. What does it mean? (See UBSD 10a.) **PARSE** ἀνέγνωτε (Mk 2:25).

8. **PARSE** γέγραπται (Mk 1:2) [The corresponding form of λύω is λέλυται – 6§7(4).], γράψαι (Mk 10:4), ἔγραψεν (Mk 10:5).

9. **PARSE** ἤρξατο (Mk 1:45), ἤρξαντο (Mk 2:23). **NOTE** that these are **NOT** from ἔρχομαι.

10. **READ** Mk 1:1-14. Can you identify the voices (active, middle or passive) of the following verbs?

γέγραπται (Mk 1:2 – see 6§7(4))
ἐξεπορεύετο (Mk 1:5 – see 6§4(3))
ἐβαπτίζοντο (Mk 1:5 – see 6§7(3) – *they were being baptized*
NOT *they were baptized* – **WHY?**
ἔρχεται (Mk 1:7 – see 6§4(3) and 6§7(2))
ἐβαπτίσθη (Mk 1:9 – see 6§9(2))
πεπλήρωται (Mk 1:15 – see 6§7(4))

11. **NOTE** that ἐγένετο occurs in Mk 1:9 and 1:11. How should it be translated in each case? See UBSD 37a.

CHAPTER SEVEN

The Greek Verb: Moods

§1 ENGLISH MOODS

In English, the verb has various moods. These reflect different ways of thinking or speaking or writing. One can make a statement or ask a question or give a command; one can make a tentative statement, testing the reaction of the person to whom one is speaking; one can express a wish or explain one's purpose; one can state a condition. Thus, "I am speaking" – "Am I speaking?" "I may speak"; "O that I could speak"; "I am speaking in order that you may learn"; "If I were to speak you might learn".

§2 SIX GREEK MOODS

(1) In Greek, the **indicative mood** is used to indicate or point out something, that is, to make a statement or ask a question.

λύω = *I loose/set free*
λύω; *Am I setting free?*

One can do this either in the present or the future or the past time.

λύσω = *I shall loose*
ἔλυσα = *I loosed.*

This can also be done in all three voices, middle and passive as well as active.

λύομαι = *I am being loosed/I am loosing myself*
ἐλύθην = *I was set free.*

(2)　The **imperative mood** is used when one gives a command.

λῦε (singular); λύετε (plural) = *loose!*

It is found not only in the second person singular and plural but also in the third person singular and plural.

λυέτω = *let him set free!* λυέτωσαν = *let them set free!*

(3)　The **infinitive mood** is not limited by person or number. It is expressed in English with the help of the small word *to*. Thus, *to speak* and *to write* are both in the infinitive mood.

λύειν = *to loose/set free*
λύεσθαι = *to be loosed/be set free/loose oneself/set oneself free*

(4)　The **participle** is a verbal adjective. It has some of the characteristics of a verb and also some of the characteristics of a noun or adjective.

The present participle in English ends in -ing; while the past participle can end in -ed. Thus, *talking* and *talked*; but *catching* and *caught*, *breaking* and *broken*.

The Greek participle similarly has various endings. The present participle active has nominative endings in -ων, – ουσα, -ον, and it is declined like adjectives – 3rd declension for the masculine and the neuter, 1st declension for the feminine.

	Masculine	Feminine	Neuter
Singular			
Nom.	λύων	λύουσα	λῦον
Voc.	λύων	λύουσα	λῦον
Acc.	λύοντα	λύουσαν	λῦον
Gen.	λύοντος	λυούσης	λύοντος
Dat.	λύοντι	λυούσῃ	λύοντι

Plural

Nom.	λύοντες	λύουσαι	λύοντα
Voc.	λύοντες	λύουσαι	λύοντα
Acc.	λύοντάς	λυούσας	λυόντα
Gen.	λυόντων	λυουσῶν	λυόντων
Dat.	λύουσι(ν)	λυούσαις	λύουσι(ν)

The aorist participle active has nominative endings in -ας, -ασα, -αν.

	Masculine	Feminine	Neuter
Singular			
Nom.	λύσας	λύσασα	λῦσαν
Voc.	λύσας	λύσασα	λῦσαν
Acc.	λύσαντα	λύσασαν	λῦσαν
Gen.	λύσαντος	λυσάσης	λύσαντος
Dat.	λύσαντι	λυσάσῃ	λύσαντι
Plural			
Nom.	λύσαντες	λύσασαι	λύσαντα
Voc.	λύσαντες	λύσασαι	λύσαντα
Acc.	λύσαντας	λυσάσας	λύσαντα
Gen.	λυσάντων	λυσασῶν	λυσάντων
Dat.	λύσασι(ν)	λυσάσαις	λύσασι(ν)

The strong aorist participle, however, has the same ending as the present participle, apart from accentuation on the first syllable of the ending. For example, βαλών, βαλοῦσα, βαλόν.

The present participle middle and passive is λυόμενος and is declined like adjectives of the second and first declensions.[1] All other middle and passive participles ending in -μενος, -μενη, -μενον[2] are declined in a similar way.

The perfect participle active has reduplication and -κ- before the endings.

---

[1] See 4§2(2) – ἀγαθός, ἀγαθή, ἀγαθόν – except that it has a recessive accent – λυόμενος, λυομένη, λυόμενον.

[2] See Appendix 1

	Masculine	Feminine	Neuter
Singular			
Nom.	λελυκώς	λελυκυῖα	λελυκός
Voc.	λελυκώς	λελυκυῖα	λελυκός
Acc.	λελυκότα	λελυκυῖαν	λελυκός
Gen.	λελυκότος	λελυκυίας	λελυκότος
Dat.	λελυκότι	λελυκυίᾳ	λελυκότι
Plural			
Nom.	λελυκότες	λελυκυῖαι	λελυκότα
Voc.	λελυκότες	λελυκυῖαι	λελυκότα
Acc.	λελυκότας	λελυκυίας	λελυκότα
Gen.	λελυκότων	λελυκυιῶν	λελυκότων
Dat.	λελυκόσι	λελυκυίαις	λελυκόσι

The aorist participle passive has nominative endings in -εις, -εισα, -εν after the -θ- characteristic of the aorist passive. It does **not** have an augment.

	Masculine	Feminine	Neuter
Singular			
Nom.	λυθείς	λυθεῖσα	λυθέν
Voc.	λυθείς	λυθεῖσα	λυθέν
Acc.	λυθέντα	λυθεῖσαν	λυθέν
Gen.	λυθέντος	λυθείσης	λυθέντος
Dat.	λυθέντι	λυθείσῃ	λυθέντι
Plural			
Nom.	λυθέντες	λυθεῖσαι	λυθέντα
Voc.	λυθέντες	λυθεῖσαι	λυθέντα
Acc.	λυθέντας	λυθεῖσας	λυθέντα
Gen.	λυθέντων	λυθεισῶν	λυθέντων
Dat.	λυθεῖσι(ν)	λυθείσαις	λυθεῖσι(ν)

(5) The **subjunctive mood** is usually found only in subordinate clauses. "I am speaking now in order that you may learn Greek" – "I was speaking last week in order that you might learn about the voices of a Greek verb". "May" or "might" would be expressed by the subjunctive mood in Greek. This mood is also used in certain conditional clauses in Greek – for example, "If I were to do this, something else would happen". In form, the subjunctive mood in Greek is characterized by lengthening of the vowel in the ending. For example, the present subjunctive active is

Person	Singular	Plural
1st	λύω	λύωμεν
2nd	λύῃς	λύητε
3rd	λύῃ	λύωσι(ν)

(6)   The sixth mood of the Greek verb is the **optative**, that is, the **wishing** mood – from the Latin **optare** = to wish. This mood is principally used to express a wish or a blessing. **O that something or other might happen!** In English, it often has an exclamation mark at the end of the sentence. The optative endings have within them a diphthong – ει/οι/αι.[3]

(7)   The negative with the indicative mood is οὐ. This becomes οὐκ before a vowel with a smooth breathing or οὐχ before an aspirate or rough breathing. The negative with all other moods is μή.[4]

§3   INDICATIVE MOOD

The indicative mood has six tenses – present, imperfect, future, aorist, perfect and pluperfect – in all three voices – active, middle and passive.

§4   IMPERATIVE MOOD

(1)   The imperative mood has three tenses – present, aorist and perfect – in all three voices. It has 3rd person singular and plural (= *let him/her/them loose*) as well as a 2nd person. There is no 1st person imperative. Instead, the 1st person of the subjunctive would be used to express exhortation (= *let me/us loose*).[5]

---

[3] See 2§5(8).

[4] See 2§6.

[5] This is the hortatory subjunctive. See 10§4(2).

(2)   The forms of the present and aorist imperatives of λύω are as follows:

	Pres. Active	Mid./Pass.
Singular		
2nd	λῦε	λύου (from λυ-εσο)
3rd	λυέτω	λυέσθω
Plural		
2nd	λύετε	λύεσθε
3rd	λυέτωσαν	λυέσθωσαν

	Aorist Active	Aorist Middle	Aorist Passive
Singular			
2nd	λῦσον	λῦσαι	λῦθητι
3rd	λυσάτω	λυσάσθω	λυθήτω
Plural			
2nd	λύσατε	λύσασθε	λύθητε
3rd	λυσάτωσαν	λυσάσθωσαν	λυθήτωσαν

(3)   The present imperative gives a command to go on doing something or other; thus, βᾶλλε λίθους = *keep on throwing stones*. The aorist imperative gives a command to do something once only; thus, βᾶλε λίθον = *throw a stone* (once). Notice that the strong aorist imperative has the same endings as the present imperative.

(4)   The perfect imperative, when required, has the same endings as for the present imperative but they are added to the perfect stem. Thus, λέλυκε, λελυκέτω, λελύκετε, λελυκέτωσαν; λέλυσο, λελύσθω, λέλυσθε, λελύσθωσαν.

(5)   The perfect imperative is very rare in the New Testament, but it does occur; e.g., πεφίμωσο (Mk 4:39) from φιμόω (= *I muzzle) – so be in a state of having been muzzled.*

§5   INFINITIVE

(1)   The infinitive has four tenses –
present: λύειν = *to keep on loosing;*
future: λύσειν = *to be about to loose;*
aorist: λῦσαι = *to loose (once);*
perfect: λελυκέναι = *to have loosed.*

(2) These also have middle and passive forms [see Appendix 1].

(3) The infinitive is used after certain verbs like δύναμαι = *I am able, I can*; ἄρχομαι = *I am beginning;* θέλω = *I wish*.

(4) The infinitivē is also used after certain impersonal verbs in the 3rd person singular: δεῖ με τοῦτο ποιεῖν = *it is necessary for me to do this*; ἔξεστί μοι τοῦτο ποιεῖν = *it is allowed to me to do this*.

(5) Verbs of ordering and beseeching can take an infinitive, as in English.

(6) ὥστε followed by the infinitive is used in Greek to express the result or consequence of an action.

(7) However, if there is stress upon the actual consequence rather than the potential result, the indicative can be used after ὥστε. In Jn 3:16, we have what has been called "the theological value of grammar". John might have written ὥστε δοῦναι = *as to give*, marking the measure of the potential gift. Instead he used the indicative "to declare the magnitude of the recorded act".[6]

(8) The infinitive can be used like a noun with the neuter definite article. In Mk 1:14, we find μετὰ τὸ παραδοθῆναι, where the last word is the aorist infinitive passive of the verb παραδίδωμι = *I betray, arrest, hand over*. The subject of the articular infinitive goes into the accusative case – so here τὸν Ἰωάννην. The articular infinitive is thus the equivalent of a ' noun – *After the arrest of John . . .*

§6 PARTICIPLES[7]

(1) The participle also has four tenses in each of its three voices. The active forms are λύων (present), λύσων (future), λύσας (aorist), λελυκώς (perfect).

[6] W.F. Howard, *Christianity according to St John* (Duckworth 1943), p.63

[7] See Chapter 8 for fuller treatment of use of participles.

(2)   The middle and passive forms of the present and perfect as well as the middle of the future and aorist and the future passive end in -μενος in the nominative singular masculine. The aorist participle passive has the characteristic θ with the ending in -εις. [See Appendix 1.]

(3)   The participle, being a verbal adjective, declines like an ordinary adjective; that is, it has three genders – masculine, feminine and neuter; five cases – nominative, vocative, accusative, genitive, dative; and two numbers – singular and plural.

(4)   The participle is used in Greek much more frequently, and with greater flexibility, than in English.

(5)   There is the adjectival use, when it qualifies a noun.[8]

> τὸν λόγον τὸν ἐσπαρμένον (Mk 4:15)
> = *the having been sown word*

(6)   The participle can also be used with a definite article without a noun as the equivalent of a noun. The article can be translated as "the person who" or "the one who" or "he who" or, if plural, "the people who" or "those who".

> ὁ σπείρων = *the sowing one*, i.e., *the sower*

(7)   When the participle is used adverbially, it is the equivalent of a clause in English. This clause can be either temporal or causal or concessive or conditional. Choice depends on the context.

(8)   The present participle expresses contemporaneous action; that is, action that is going on at the same time as the action of the verb in the main clause.

(9)   The aorist participle is used to describe previous action; that is, action that precedes that of the main verb.

(10)   An exception to this rule is the very common expression –

---

[8] See 8§3.

ἀποκριθεὶς εἶπεν
having answered he said/he answered and said/in answer he said

§7 SUBJUNCTIVE MOOD

(1)   The subjunctive is used in a subordinate clause after ἵνα
to express purpose.

λέγω ἵνα μανθάνητε τὴν κοινήν (διάλεκτον)
*I am speaking in order that/so that you may learn the common
Greek (dialect).*

(2)   Since the negative with the subjunctive is μή, a clause
introduced by ἵνα μή could be rendered into English either
as *in order that . . . not . . .* or as *lest . . . .*

γρηγορεῖτε καὶ προσεύχεσθε ἵνα μὴ εἰσέλθητε εἰς πειρασμόν
*watch and pray so that you may not, (or, lest you) enter into
temptation (Mt.26:41)*

§8   OPTATIVE MOOD

The most common optative in Paul is

μὴ γένοιτο
May it not happen!
Of course not!
No! No! (NEB)
God forbid! (AV)[9]

§9   QUESTIONS

(1)   Unless they are deliberative,[10] questions are expressed in
Greek in the indicative mood with a question mark similar to
a semi-colon at the end of the sentence.[11]

[9] See 2§5(8).

[10] See 10§4(3).

[11] See 1§25.

(2) Hesitant questions, where the questioner is in doubt about the answer and wishes to show that doubt, are introduced by μή or μήτι.

Μήτι οὗτός ἐστιν ὁ υἱὸς Δαυίδ; (Mt.12:23)
Is this man perhaps the son of David?

(3) Questions expecting the answer "no" are also introduced by μή or μήτι.

Μήτι ἔρχεται ὁ λύχνος ἵνα ὑπὸ τὴν κλίνην τεθῇ; (Mk 4:21)
Does the light come so that it may be placed under the bed?

(4) Questions expecting the answer "yes" are introduced by οὐ/οὐκ/οὐχ or οὐχί.

οὐχ (ἔρχεται ὁ λύχνος) ἵνα ἐπὶ τὴν λυχνίαν τεθῇ; (Mk 4:21)
Is it not so that it may be placed upon the lampstand?

Without the question mark this would mean: *The light does not come so that it may be placed upon the lampstand.*

οὐχὶ δύο στρουθία ἀσσαρίου πωλεῖται; (Mt.10:29)[12]
Are not two sparrows being put on sale for an assarion?

ASSIGNMENTS

1. SEE Appendix 2. **WRITE DOWN and LEARN** the principal parts of διδάσκω, δίδωμι, ἔρχομαι, ἐσθίω, εὑρίσκω.

2. **PARSE** δοθήσεται (Mk 8:12).[13]

3. **PARSE** ἔρχεται (Mk 1:7), προσελθών (Mk 1:31)[14],

---

[12] Lk.12:6, where five are sold for two assaria. Yet the fifth sparrow is not forgotten by God. See 3§5(2)n4.

[13] Remember that the future passive can be derived from the aorist passive – see 5§2(1).

[14] Remember that strong aorist participles are declined like present participles – 7§2(4), pp.63f.

ἤρχοντο (Mk 1:45), ἤρχετο (Mk 2:13), συνέρχεται (Mk 3:20), ἐξῆλθον (Mk 8:11), ἀπῆλθεν (Mk 8:13).

4. **PARSE** ἐσθίων (Mk 1:6), ἔφαγεν (Mk 2:26), ἔφαγον (Mk 8:8).

5. **PARSE** εὗρον (Mk 1:37), εὗρεν (Mk 7:30).

6. **STUDY carefully** the use of the various Greek moods as illustrated in the following sentences. **TRANSLATE** each sentence into English, making sure that you can parse each verb as you do so.

Indicative

(1) ἀποστέλλω τὸν ἄγγελόν μου πρὸ προσώπου σου. (Mk 1:2)

(2) ἐγὼ ἐβάπτισα ὑμᾶς ὕδατι, αὐτὸς δὲ ὑμᾶς βαπτίσει ἐν πνεύματι ἁγίῳ. (Mk 1:8)

Imperative

(3) ἑτοιμάσατε τὴν ὁδὸν κυρίου. (Mk 1:3)

Infinitive

(4) ἤρξατο διδάσκειν αὐτοὺς ὅτι δεῖ τὸν υἱὸν τοῦ ἀνθρώπου πολλὰ παθεῖν. (Mk 8:31)

(5) δύνασθε πιεῖν τὸ ποτήριον ὃ ἐγὼ πίνω; (Mk 10:38)

(6) οὐ θέλετε ἐλθεῖν πρός με. (Jn 5:40)

(7) Οὐκ ἔξεστίν σοι ἔχειν τὴν γυναῖκα τοῦ ἀδελφοῦ σου. (Mk 6:18)

(8) παραγγέλλει τῷ ὄχλῳ ἀναπεσεῖν ἐπὶ τῆς γῆς. (Mk 8:6)

(9) ἐθεράπευσεν αὐτόν, ὥστε τὸν κωφὸν λαλεῖν καὶ βλέπειν. (Mt.12:22)

(10) Οὕτως γὰρ ἠγάπησεν ὁ θεὸς τὸν κόσμον ὥστε τὸν υἱὸν τὸν μονογενῆ ἔδωκεν. (Jn 3:16)[15]

(11) Μετὰ δὲ τὸ παραδοθῆναι τὸν ᾽Ιωάννην ἦλθεν ὁ ᾽Ιησοῦς εἰς τὴν Γαλιλαίαν. (Mk 1:14)

Participles

(12) ἐγένετο ᾽Ιωάννης βαπτίζων καὶ κηρύσσων. (Mk 1:4)

(13) ἐβαπτίζοντο ὑπ᾽ αὐτοῦ . . . ἐξομολογούμενοι τὰς ἁμαρτίας αὐτῶν. (Mk 1:5)

(14) ὁ υἱός σου οὗτος ὁ καταφαγών σου τὸν βίον μετὰ πορνῶν ἦλθεν. (Lk.15:30)

(15) ὁ πιστεύων εἰς ἐμὲ οὐ πιστεύει εἰς ἐμὲ ἀλλὰ εἰς τὸν πέμψαντά με. (Jn 12:44)

(16) ἰδοὺ ἐξῆλθεν ὁ σπείρων σπεῖραι. (Mk 4:3)

(17) Οὐ χρείαν ἔχουσιν οἱ ἰσχύοντες ἰατροῦ ἀλλ᾽ οἱ κακῶς ἔχοντες. (Mk 2:17)

(18) ταῦτα εἰπὼν ᾽Ιησοῦς ἐταράχθη. (Jn 13:21)

(19) οἱ μαθηταὶ αὐτοῦ ἤρξαντο ὁδὸν ποιεῖν τίλλοντες τοὺς στάχυας. (Mk 2:23)

Subjunctive

(20) οὐ θέλετε ἐλθεῖν πρός με ἵνα ζωὴν ἔχητε. (Jn 5:40)

Optative

(21) Μηκέτι εἰς τὸν αἰῶνα ἐκ σοῦ μηδεὶς καρπὸν φάγοι. (Mk 11:14)

---

[15] Note that the infinitive is *not* used here. See 7§5(7).

CHAPTER EIGHT

The Use of Participles in Greek

§1 FREQUENCY OF PARTICIPLES INGREEK

(1) Participles are used far more frequently in Greek than they are in English.

(2) In translating a participle from Greek into English, therefore, it may often be necessary to use a relative clause ("who", "which") or an adverbial clause.

§2 ADVERBIAL CLAUSES IN ENGLISH

(1) The adverbial clause may be causal ("because") or concessive ("although") or conditional ("if") or, most frequently, temporal ("while"/"after"/"when"). The context will usually indicate which is the most appropriate rendering.

(2) Thus, ταῦτα ποιήσαντες μακάριοι ἔσεσθε could be rendered into English as

Having done these things you will be happy
or
Because/although/if/after/when you have done these things you will be happy.

§3 ATTRIBUTIVE POSITION

A participle can be used like an attributive adjective.[1]

---

[1] See 4§5.

ἄξιόν ἐστιν τὸ ἀρνίον τὸ ἐσφαγμένον λαβεῖν τὴν δύναμιν.
(Rev. 5:12)
Worthy is the lamb **the one having been slain** *to receive power.*

Notice the presence-of the neuter definite article twice.

§4 PERIPHRASTIC TENSE

A participle can be used as part of a periphrastic tense along
with part of the verb *to be* or *to become.*

ἦν ὁ Ἰωάννης ἐνδεδύμενος τρίχας καμήλου. (Mk 1:6)
John was in the state of having been clothed or *of having clothed*
himself in hairs of a camel.

[ἦν is 3rd person singular of imperfect of verb *to be* used
along with the perfect participle middle or passive of ἐνδύω =
I clothe.]

ἐγένετο Ἰωάννης βαπτίζων ἐν τῇ ἐρήμῳ. (Mk 1:4)
John arose/was baptizing in the desert.

ἦσαν δέ τινες τῶν γραμματέων ἐκεῖ καθήμενοι. (Mk 2:6)
Some of the scribes were sitting there.

§5 PARTICIPLE AS NOUN

A participle can be used with or without a definite article as
the equivalent of a noun.

φωνὴ βοῶντος ἐν τῇ ἐρήμῳ (Mk 1:3)
A voice of one crying[2] *in the desert*

ἰδοὺ ἐξῆλθεν ὁ σπείρων σπεῖραι (Mk 4:3)
Behold the sowing one/the sower went out to sow

---

[2] Note carefully that this present participle is in the genitive case. So it is not
a voice crying but a voice of one crying/shouting out.

§6   ADVERBIAL USAGE

Most frequently, the Greek participle is used adverbially and may have to be translated into English by an adverbial clause.

§7   TENSE OF THE PARTICIPLE

(1)   The tense of the participle must be carefully noted.

(2)   The present participle signifies action contemporaneous with, or simultaneous to, the action of the main verb.

Καὶ παράγων παρὰ τὴν θάλασσαν . . . εἶδεν Σίμωνα. . . . (Mk 1:16)
And while going along beside the sea . . . he saw Simon.

(3)   The aorist participle is used to express action previous to that of the main verb.

καὶ περιβλεψάμενος αὐτοὺς μετ’ ὀργῆς . . . λέγει τῷ ἀνθρώπῳ . . . . (Mk 3:5)
And when he had looked around them with anger . . . he said to the person/man . . . .[3]

§8   GENITIVE ABSOLUTE

(1)   The participle can agree with the subject, or the object, or the indirect object of a clause.

(2)   When it does not agree with any of these, it is put into the genitive case. This is known as **the genitive absolute**.

’Οψίας γενομένης (Mk 1:32)
When evening had come

γενομένης θλίψεως (Mk 4:17)
tribulation having arisen

καὶ ἐσθιόντων αὐτῶν (Mk 14:22)
and while they were eating

[3] For the historic present, see 3§15(7)n11.

ASSIGNMENTS

1. **SEE** Appendix 2. **WRITE DOWN and LEARN** the principal parts of κηρύσσω, λαμβάνω, λέγω, μανθάνω, ὁράω.

2. **PARSE** κηρύσσων (Mk 1:4), ἐκήρυσσεν (Mk 1:7), κηρύξω (Mk 1:38), κηρύσσειν (Mk 1:45), ἐκήρυξαν (Mk 6:12), ἐκήρυσσον (Mk 7:36).

3. **PARSE** λαμβάνουσιν (Mk 4:16), λαβών (Mk 6:41), λαβεῖν (Mk 7:27).

4. **PARSE** λέγων (Mk 1:7), λέγοντας (Mk 1:27), λέγουσιν (Mk 1:30), λέγει (Mk 2:10), ἔλεγον (Mk 2:16).

5. **PARSE** μάθετε (Mk 13:28).

6. **PARSE** ὅρα (Mk 1:44), ὁρᾶτε (Mk 8:15), ὁρῶ (Mk 8:24), ὤφθη (Mk 9:4), ὄψονται (Mk 13:26).[4]

7. **EXPLAIN and TRANSLATE** the following phrases:

(1)   ἀκούσασα περὶ τοῦ ᾽Ιησοῦ . . . (Mk 5:27)

(2)   καὶ γενομένης ἡμέρας εὐκαίρου . . . (Mk 6:21)

(3)   καὶ ἤδη ὥρας πολλῆς γενομένης . . . (Mk 6:35)

(4)   καὶ ἰδόντες τινὰς τῶν μαθητῶν . . . (Mk 7:2)

(5)   καὶ προσκαλεσάμενος πάλιν τὸν ὄχλον . . . (Mk 7:14)

8. **READ** carefully Mk 5:2. **NOTE** the phrase in the genitive absolute.

> καὶ ἐξελθόντος αὐτοῦ ἐκ τοῦ πλοίου (Mk 5:2)
> *And when he had come out of the ship . . . .*

This genitive absolute could have been put into the dative case. Why?

[4] See 5§9(4).

CHAPTER NINE

The Greek Infinitive

§1 MEANING OF INFINITIVE

The infinitive mood is not limited by person or number. It is expressed in English with the help of the small word "to". Thus, **to speak** and **to write** are both in the infinitive mood. So in Greek λύειν = *to loose/set free*.

§2 TENSES OF THE GREEK INFINITIVE

The infinitive has four tenses in each of the three voices:

	Active	Middle	Passive
present	λύειν	λύεσθαι	λύεσθαι
future	λύσειν	λύσεσθαι	λυθήσεσθαι
aorist	λῦσαι	λύσασθαι	λυθῆναι
perfect	λελυκέναι	λελύσθαι	λελύσθαι

§3 AORIST INFINITIVE WITHOUT AUGMENT

(1) While the perfect infinitives have reduplication, the aorist infinitives do *not* have augments. Remember that the aorist is a historic tense only in the indicative mood.

(2) This means that the time of the action is less important than its aspect. In other words, while the present infinitive is used with reference to continuous or repeated action, the aorist infinitive is punctiliar and signifies a single action without reference to time.

§4   INFINITIVE OF VERB "TO BE"

The infinitive of εἰμί is εἶναι = *to be*.

§5   NEGATIVE WITH INFINITIVE

The negative with the infinitive is μή.

§6   INFINITIVE AFTER CERTAIN VERBS

The infinitive is used after certain verbs:

δύναμαι	*I am able/I can*
ἄρχομαι	*I begin*[1]
θέλω	*I wish*.

Οὐδεὶς δύναται δυσὶ κυρίοις δουλεύειν. (Mt.6:24)
No-one can be a slave to two masters.

Ἐὰν θέλῃς δύνασαί με καθαρίσαι. (Mk 1:40)
[Note carefully which is the infinitive here!]
If you wish you can cleanse me.

ὁ δὲ ἐξελθὼν ἤρξατο κηρύσσειν πολλά. (Mk 1:45)
But when he had gone out he began to proclaim many things.

καὶ εἰσελθὼν εἰς οἰκίαν οὐδένα ἤθελεν γνῶναι. (Mk 7:24)
*And when he had gone into a house/home he was not wishing
anyone to know.*

ἤθελον οὖν λαβεῖν αὐτὸν εἰς τὸ πλοῖον. (Jn 6:21)
Therefore they were wishing to receive him into the ship.

§7   INFINITIVE WITH IMPERSONAL VERBS

The infinitive is also used after certain impersonal verbs in the
3rd person singular.

[1] See 6§6(2).

δεῖ[2] με τοῦτο ποιεῖν
It is necessary for me to do this.

ἔξεστί μοι τοῦτο ποιεῖν.
It is allowed to me/lawful for me to do this.

οὐκ ἔξεστίν σοι ἔχειν τὴν γυναῖκα τοῦ ἀδελφοῦ σου.
(Mk 6:18)
It is not lawful for you to have the wife of your brother.

Notice that δεῖ is followed by the accusative and infinitive while ἔξεστιν usually occurs with the dative case but can also be followed by the accusative.

. . . οὕς οὐκ ἔξεστιν φαγεῖν εἰ μὴ τοὺς ἱερεῖς. (Mk 2:26)
. . . which it is allowed to eat only [to] the priests; i.e., which only the priests are allowed to eat.

§8 ORDERING AND BESEECHING

Verbs of ordering and beseeching can take an infinitive.

Διδάσκαλε, δέομαί σου ἐπιβλέψαι ἐπὶ τὸν υἱόν μου. (Lk.9:38)
Teacher, I beg you to look upon my son.

§9 CONSEQUENCE OR RESULT

(1) ὥστε followed by the infinitive is used in Greek to express the result or consequence of an action. Notice that ὥστε is made up of ὥς meaning *thus* or *so* and -τε, which is an enclitic[3] meaning *and*. This should help you to remember that ὥστε introduces the consequence or result of an action.

---

[2] δέω can be used as a normal verb meaning *bind* or *tie*; see UBSD 40a and 41a. So when used impersonally, δεῖ με means *it is binding on me*. For the aorist infinitive of δέω, see Mk 5:3 – δῆσαι; for the aorist indicative, see Mk 6:17 – ἔδησεν; and for the aorist subjunctive, see Mk 3:27 – δήσῃ. Remember that it is an -εω contracted verb.

[3] See 3§6(5).

καὶ συνήχθησαν πολλοὶ ὥστε μηκέτι χωρεῖν μηδὲ τὰ πρὸς τὴν
θύραν. (Mk 2:2)
*And many gathered with the result that not even the things
towards the door were making room.*[4]

(2)   However, if there is stress upon the actual consequence
rather than the potential result, the indicative can be used after
ὥστε, as in Jn 3:16.[5]

§10   ARTICULAR INFINITIVE[6]

(1)   The infinitive can be used like a noun with the neuter
definite article. This is called **the articular infinitive.**

(2)   It is sometimes said that the subject of the infinitive goes
into the accusative case, but it is more correct to call this an
accusative of respect or an accusative of reference.

(3)   The articular infinitive is often found after prepositions
such as μετά, πρός, ἐν, διά.

Μετὰ τὸ παραδοθῆναι τὸν Ἰωάννην ἦλθεν ὁ Ἰησοῦς.
(Mk 1:14)

Note the aorist infinitive passive of the verb παραδίδωμι[7] = *I
betray, arrest, hand over.* The "subject" of the articular infinitive
is in the accusative case. The articular infinitive is thus the
equivalent of a noun – *After the arrest of John . . . .*

§11   PURPOSE

The infinitive can be used to express purpose either on its own

---

[4] The phrase τὰ πρὸς τὴν θύραν is either an accusative of respect (*there was
no longer room not even in respect of the things towards the door*) or it is the
subject of the infinitive χωρεῖν.

[5] See 7§5(8).

[6] See 7§5(7).

[7] See 11§4; cf. λυθῆναι (Appendix 1).

or preceded by τοῦ or by a preposition such as εἰς or πρός along with the accusative singular neuter of the definite article.

οὐκ ἦλθον καλέσαι δικαίους ἀλλὰ ἁμαρτωλούς. (Mk 2:17)
I did not come to call righteous people but sinners.

ἐζήτουν κατὰ τοῦ 'Ιησοῦ μαρτυρίαν εἰς τὸ θανατῶσαι αὐτόν. (Mk 14:55)
They were seeking evidence against Jesus to put him to death.

§12 ΓΙΝΕΤΑΙ with ACCUSATIVE AND INFINITIVE

γίνεται/ἐγένετο is sometimes followed by an accusative and infinitive.

καὶ γίνεται κατακεῖσθαι αὐτὸν ἐν τῇ οἰκίᾳ αὐτοῦ. (Mk 2:15)
And it happened that he was reclining at table in his house.[8]

καὶ ἐγένετο αὐτὸν ἐν τοῖς σάββασιν παραπορεύεσθαι διὰ τῶν σπορίμων. (Mk 2:23)
And it happened that on the Sabbath he was going through the grainfields

§13 ΠΡΙΝ with ACCUSATIVE AND INFINITIVE

πρίν or πρὶν ἤ (= *before*) is followed by an accusative and infinitive.

Πρὶν [ἤ] ἀλέκτορα φωνῆσαι δὶς τρίς με ἀπαρνήσῃ. (Mk 14:30,72)
Before the cock has crowed twice thrice you will disown me.

§14 ASPECT NOT TIME

Remember that the tense of the infinitive expresses aspect rather than time.[9]

---

[8] Note the historic present – see 3§14(7)n8.

[9] See 9§3(2).

ASSIGNMENTS

1. **SEE** Appendix 2. **WRITE DOWN and LEARN** the principal parts of πάσχω, πέμπω, πίνω, πίπτω.

2. **PARSE**
(1) παθοῦσα (Mk 5:26), παθεῖν (Mk 8:31), πάθη (Mk 9:12);
(2) πέμψον (Mk 5:12);
(3) ἐσθίει (Mk 2:16), πιεῖν (Mk 10:38);
(4) ἔπεσεν (Mk 4:4), πίπτει (Mk 5:22).

3. Ἐαν θέλῃς δύνασαί με καθαρίσαι. (Mk 1:40) **PARSE** each of the verbs in this sentence. [Note carefully which is the infinitive.]

4. **TRANSLATE into English:**

(1) δεῖ τὸν υἱὸν τοῦ ἀνθρώπου πολλὰ παθεῖν. (Mk 8:31)

(2) ἔξεστιν τοῖς σάββασιν ἀγαθὸν ποιῆσαι; (Mk 3:4)
[Note the significance of the dative here.]

(3) μετὰ τὸ ἐγερθῆναί με προάξω ὑμᾶς εἰς τὴν Γαλιλαίαν. (Mk 14:28)

(4) καὶ ἐγένετο ἐν τῷ σπείρειν . . . (Mk 4:4)

(5) διὰ τὸ μὴ ἔχειν ῥίζαν ἐξηράνθη. (Mk 4:6)

(6) συνέρχεται πάλιν ὄχλος ὥστε μὴ δύνασθαι αὐτοὺς μηδὲ ἄρτον φαγεῖν. (Mk 3:20)

5. ΞΗΡΑΙΝΩ

(1) **PARSE** ἐξηράνθη (Mk 4:6).

(2) **SEE** Mk 3:1 for another example of this same verb. Can you parse it also?[10]

(3) The verb is ξηραίνω. Look it up in UBSD. What is the adjective from the same root? See Mk 3:3.

---

[10] Note that when a verb begins with a double consonant or with σ + one or more consonants reduplication in the perfect tense takes the form of ἐ- as for the augment. For other perfect formations, see 2§8(14), 2§10(7). Cf. also ἔσταλκα from στέλλω and ἐσπαρμένον (Mk 4:15) from σπείρω.

CHAPTER TEN

Uses of The Subjunctive Mood

§1 LENGTHENING IN ENDINGS

Subjunctives are formed by lengthening the first vowel in the endings of the present indicative active and middle/passive and writing subscript any iota. These endings are used for aorist subjunctives by inserting -σ- for active and middle. Aorist passives are formed by inserting -θ- before the present endings.

§2 TWO TENSES

In the New Testament, there are **two tenses** of the subjunctive mood in all three voices.

Present and Aorist Subjunctives

	Active	Middle	Passive
Present	λύω	λύωμαι	λύωμαι
	λύῃς	λύῃ	λύῃ
	λύῃ	λύηται	λύηται
	λύωμεν	λυώμεθα	λυώμεθα
	λύητε	λύησθε	λύησθε
	λύωσι(ν)	λύωνται	λύωνται
Aorist	λύσω	λύσωμαι	λυθῶ
	λύσῃς	λύσῃ	λυθῇς
	λύσῃ	λύσηται	λυθῇ
	λύσωμεν	λυσώμεθα	λυθῶμεν
	λύσητε	λύσησθε	λυθῆτε
	λύσωσι(ν)	λύσωνται	λυθῶσι(ν)

NOTE: There is no future subjunctive in Greek. What loo' ⌄ like a future with -σ- is **aorist**.

§3 SUBJUNCTIVE OF 'EIMI

The subjunctive of εἰμί = endings of present subjunctive active of λύω.

ὦ ᾖς ᾖ ὦμεν ἦτε ὦσι(ν).

§4 EIGHT MAIN USES OF SUBJUNCTIVE

There are **eight main uses** of the subjunctive mood in Greek.

(1) STRONG PROHIBITION

Emphatic denial or **strong prohibition** is expressed by μή with the aorist subjunctive.

καὶ μὴ εἰσενέγκῃς ἡμᾶς εἰς πειρασμόν. (Mt.6:13)
And do not lead us into temptation.

ὅρα μηδενὶ μηδὲν εἴπῃς. (Mk 1:44)[1]
See that to no-one nothing you say!
[How should this be expressed in English?]

(2) HORTATORY SUBJUNCTIVE

Exhortation is expressed by 1st person subjunctive.

ἄγωμεν ἀλλαχοῦ εἰς τὰς ἐχομένας κωμοπόλεις. (Mk 1:38)
Let us go elsewhere into the neighbouring country towns.

ἐγείρεσθε, ἄγωμεν ἐντεῦθεν. (Jn. 14:31)
Rise, let us go from here.

φάγωμεν καὶ πίωμεν, αὔριον γὰρ ἀποθνῄσκομεν.
(1 Cor.15:32)
Let us eat and let us drink, for tomorrow we die.

(3) DELIBERATIVE SUBJUNCTIVE

Deliberation can be expressed by subjunctive though future indicative can also be used.

---

[1] Notice the double negative here. See 2§6(4) and (5).

Πῶς ὁμοιώσωμεν τὴν βασιλείαν τοῦ θεοῦ; (Mk 4:30)
How are we to compare the reign/kingdom of God?

Ἀπελθόντες ἀγοράσωμεν δηναρίων διακοσίων ἄρτους καὶ
δώσομεν αὐτοῖς φαγεῖν; (Mk 6:37)
*Having gone away are we to buy loaves worth two hundred
denarii and shall we give to them to eat?*

δῶμεν ἢ μὴ δῶμεν; (Mk 12:14)
Are we to give or are we not to give?

(4) EMPHATIC NEGATIVE FUTURE

An **emphatic negative future** is expressed by means of οὐ μή
and the aorist subjunctive.

οὐ μὴ ἀφεθῇ ὧδε λίθος ἐπὶ λίθον ὃς οὐ μὴ καταλυθῇ.
(Mk 13:2)
*A stone will not be placed here upon a stone which will not be
torn down.*[2]

ὁ οὐρανὸς καὶ ἡ γῆ παρελεύσεται, οἱ δὲ λόγοι μου οὐ μὴ
παρέλθωσιν. (Mt.24:34)
*Heaven and earth will pass away, but my words will not pass
away.*

(5) PURPOSE or FINAL CLAUSE

Purpose can be expressed by means of ἵνα or ὅπως along
with the subjunctive.

ἐποίησεν δώδεκα ἵνα ὦσιν μετ' αὐτοῦ . . . . (Mk 3:14)
He made (appointed) twelve so that they might be with him.

(6) IMPERATIVAL ἵνα

The **imperatival** ἵνα is an extension of this usage that developed

---

[2] This is a fairly literal translation which needs to be expressed more
idiomatically in English. How do various modern versions deal with this
saying?

by the 1st century A.D. and is used at least 18 or 19 times in the New Testament.[3]

ἵνα ἐλθὼν ἐπιθῇς τὰς χεῖρας αὐτῇ ἵνα σωθῇ καὶ ζήσῃ.
(Mk 5:23)
Having come, lay your hands upon her so that she may be saved and live.
(Cf. Mt.9:18 – ἐλθὼν ἐπίθες τὴν χεῖρά σου ἐπ' αὐτήν.)[4]

'Ραββουνί, ἵνα ἀναβλέψω. (Mk 10:51)
Rabbi, let me recover my sight!
ἀλλ' ἵνα πληρωθῶσιν αἱ γραφαί. (Mk 14:49)
But let the scriptures be fulfilled!

ἀλλ' ἵνα φανερωθῇ τὰ ἔργα τοῦ θεοῦ ἐν αὐτῷ. (Jn 9:3)
But let the works of God be made clear in him.

(7) INDEFINITE CLAUSES

Indefinite clauses (*whoever, whenever, wherever, until*) are expressed with the subjunctive and sometimes have ἄν or ἐάν inserted into them.

ὅπου ἐὰν εἰσέλθητε εἰς οἰκίαν, ἐκεῖ μένετε ἕως ἄν ἐξέλθητε ἐκεῖθεν. (Mk. 6:10)
Wherever you enter into a house, remain there until you go out from there.

ὃς γὰρ ἐὰν θέλῃ τὴν ψυχὴν αὐτοῦ σῶσαι ἀπολέσει αὐτήν. (Mk 8:35)
For whoever wishes to save his life will lose it.

---

[3] See W.G. Morrice, *The Imperatival* ἵνα in *The Bible Translator* vol.23 (1972), pp.326–330; cf. J.H. Moulton, *A Grammar of New Testament Greek* vol.4: Style by Nigel Turner (T. & T. Clark 1976), pp.23,73,151. Professor Cranfield is less confident than I am about the occurrences of the imperatival ἵνα. He feels that "the argument for it is stronger in some of the examples than in others". He continues: "I'm inclined to hold to the view that in Mk 14:49 something like γέγονεν should be understood. And something similar in Jn 9:3."

[4] Notice that Matthew changes Mark's imperatival ἵνα construction into a straightforward aorist imperative.

(8) CONDITIONAL CLAUSES

Conditional clauses in certain cases contain a verb in the subjunctive mood.

§5 CONDITIONAL SENTENCES

(1)   Conditional sentences (past, present or future) can express either a real or a potential (i.e., unfulfilled or indistinct) condition.

(2)   The *if* clause is the protasis (from προτείνω = *stretch before*) while the main clause is known as the apodosis (from ἀποδίδωμι = *give back*).

(3)   The mood in most conditional sentences is indicative (occasionally imperative in apodosis).

(4)   In future conditional sentences, however, ἐάν plus the subjunctive can be used in the protasis of real conditions (**Type 3**) and the optative is used in potential conditions in both clauses (**Type 6**).

(5)   Since conditional sentences are rare in Mark or even in the New Testament as a whole, the accompanying table is given mainly for reference purposes.

(6)   Mt. 19:17 contains an example of **Type 2,** though instead of the present indicative in the apodosis there is an aorist imperative.

εἰ θέλεις εἰς τὴν ζωὴν εἰσελθεῖν, τήρησον τὰς ἐντολάς.
If you wish to enter into life, keep the commandments.

(7)   Mk 1:40 contains an example of **Type 3:**[5]

Ἐὰν θέλῃς δύνασαί με καθαρίσαι.
[Note present here – not the future.]

---

[5] Other examples are Jn 6:51; 15:10.

If you are (or *shall be*) *willing, you are able* (present tense) *to cleanse me.*

(8)   Note that the sign of the potential is ἄν in the principal clause or apodosis, stressing the contingent nature of the statement (**Types 4** to **6**).

(9)   **Type 6** is not fully employed in the New Testament. In 1 Pet.3:14 and 17, the apodosis occurs in a different form from what might be expected.

ἀλλ' εἰ καὶ πάσχοιτε διὰ δικαιοσύνην, μακάριοι. (1 Pet.3:14)
But if you should suffer on account of righteousness, happy are you

. . . εἰ θέλοι τὸ θέλημα τοῦ θεοῦ . . . (1 Pet.3:17)
. . . if the will of God should wish . . .

CONDITIONAL SENTENCES		
	Protasis	*Apodosis*
REAL CONDITIONS		
Type 1 Past	εἰ τοῦτο ἐποίεις/ἐποίησας *If you were doing/did this,*	ἡμάρτανες/ἥμαρτες *you were sinning/ sinned.*
Rule:	Past indic. (imperf. or aorist)	in both clauses
Type 2 Present	εἰ τοῦτο ποιεῖς *If you are doing this,*	ἁμαρτάνεις *you are sinning.*
Rule:	Present indicative	in both clauses

CONDITIONAL SENTENCES

Protasis	Apodosis
REAL CONDITIONS	

Type 3 Future	εἰ τοῦτο ποιήσεις OR ἐὰν τοῦτο ποιῇς/ ποιησῇς *If you do [shall do] this,*	ἁμαρτήσεις *you will be sinning.*
Rule:	Future indicative or, more frequently, ἐάν + pres./aor. subj. in protasis	in both clauses

POTENTIAL CONDITIONS	

Type 4 Past	εἰ τοῦτο ἐποίεις/ἐποίησας *If you were doing/had done this,*	ἡμάρτανες/ἥμαρτες ἄν *you would have sinned*
Rule:	Past indicative in both;	ἄν in apodosis
Type 5 Present	εἰ τοῦτο ἐποίεις *If you were doing this [now],*	ἡμάρτανες ἄν. *you would be sinning.*
Rule:	Imperfect indicative in both;	ἄν in apodosis.
Type 6 Future	εἰ τοῦτο ποιοίης *If you should do this,*	ἁμαρτάνοις ἄν. *you would be sinning.*
Rule:	Optative in both;	ἄν in apodosis

ASSIGNMENTS

1. **SEE** Appendix 2. **WRITE DOWN and LEARN** the principal parts of τρέχω and φέρω.

2. **PARSE** συνέδραμον (Mk 6:33), περιέδραμον (Mk 6:55).[6]

3. **PARSE** ἐνέγκαι (Mk 6:27), ἐξήνεγκεν (Mk 8:23).[7]

4. **IDENTIFY, EXPLAIN, PARSE and TRANSLATE** all the subjunctives in

(1)   Mk 1:38 (2);

(2)   Mk 1:40 (1);

(3)   Mk 1:44 (1);

(4)   Mk 2:10 (1);

(5)   Mk 2:20 (1);

(6)   Mk 3:2 (1);

(7)   Mk 3:6 (1);

(8)   Mk 3:9 (2);

(9)   Mk 3:10 (1);

(10) Mk 3:12 (1);

(11) Mk 3:14 (2);

(12) Mk 3:24 (1);

(13) Mk 3:25 (1);

(14) Mk 3:27 (1);

(15) Mk 3:28 (1);

(16) Mk 3:29 (1);

(17) Mk 3:35 (1).

[6] See 5§9(5).

[7] See 5§9(6).

CHAPTER ELEVEN

Second Conjugation Verbs

§1 VERBS ENDING IN – MI

Second conjugation verbs are distinguished from those of the first by the ending of the first person singular of the present indicative active. Instead of ending in -ω, these verbs end in -μι. They differ from first conjugation verbs mainly in the present, imperfect and aorist tenses.

§2 FOUR VERBAL STEMS

Four very common -μι verbs have verbal stems δο (= *give*), θε (= *place*), στα (= *stand*) and ἑ or ἡ (= *send*).

§3 REDUPLICATED PRESENT STEMS

In each case, the present stem (from which are derived present and imperfect tenses[1]) has reduplication – διδο, τιθε, ἱστα and ἱη. Notice in the case of the third, reduplication takes the form of the rough breathing (rather than σ) along with ι, while in the case of the fourth, reduplication takes place with the aid of ι and the loss of the aspirate on the stem.

---

[1] See 5§2(1).

§4 PRINCIPAL PARTS

The principal parts of these four verbs are:

δίδωμι	δώσω	ἔδωκα	δέδωκα	δέδομαι	ἐδόθην
τίθημι	θήσω	ἔθηκα	τέθεικα	τέθειμαι	ἐτέθην
ἵστημι	στήσω	ἔστην ἔστησα	ἕστηκα	ἕσταμαι	ἐστάθην
-ἵημι	-ἥσω	-ἧκα²	-εἷκα	-ἕωμαι³	-ἕθην

§5 -IHMI in COMPOUNDS

The fourth of these verbs is found only in compounds.[4] Those in Mark are [examples from Mk 1–8 only]:

ἀφίημι	*send away*	Mk 8:13
	forgive	Mk 2:5,7,9,10; 3:28; 4:12
	permit	Mk 1:34; 5:19,37; 7:12,27
	leave behind	Mk 1:18,20,31; 4:36; 7:8; 8:13
συνίημι	*bring together*	Mk 4:12; 6:52; 7:14; 8:17,21
	understand	

§6 AORIST FORMS

(1)   Particular attention should be given to the forms of the aorist active. Notice that those of δίδωμι, τίθημι and -ἵημι are in -κ- rather than in -σ-. However, they are easily distinguishable from the perfect forms, which have reduplication; but watch the difference between -ἧκα (aorist) and -εἷκα (perfect).

---

[2] See Mt.6:12 – ἄφες ἡμῖν . . . ὡς καὶ ἡμεῖς ἀφήκαμεν . . . .

[3] The only form of this perfect passive found in the NT is the 3rd person plural – ἀφέωνται as a variant reading in Mk 2:5; cf. Lk.7:48.

[4] See 2§11.

See Mk 1:31; 5:19, 37 for ἀφῆκεν.
See Mk 2:26; 4:7; 6:28 for ἔδωκεν.
See Mk 6:29 for ἔθηκαν; Mk 8:25 for ἔθηκεν.

(2) The 1st aorist of τίθημι is found only in the indicative.
Other moods have 2nd aorist forms.

(3) Aorist imperatives are θές, θέτω, θέτε, θέτωσαν.

(4) Aorist infinitives are θεῖναι (active), θέσθαι (middle) and
τεθῆναι (passive).

(5) Aorist participles active are θείς, θεῖσα, θέν (gen. θέντος,
θείσης, θέντος – active).

§7 PRESENT INDICATIVE ACTIVE

Present Indicative Active Tenses are:

δίδωμι	τίθημι	ἵστημι	-ἵημι
δίδως	τίθης	ἵστης	-ἵης
δίδωσι(ν)	τίθησι(ν)	ἵστησι(ν)	-ἵησι(ν)
δίδομεω	τίθεμεν	ἵσταμεν	-ἵεμεν[5]
δίδοτε	τίθετε	ἵστατε	-ἵετε
διδόασι(ν)	τιθέασι(ν)	ἱστᾶσι(ν)	-ἵασι(ν)

§8 PRESENT INDICATIVE MIDDLE AND PASSIVE

Present Indicative Middle and Passive Tenses are:

δίδομαι	τίθεμαι	ἵσταμαι
δίδοσαι	τίθεσαι	ἵστασαι
δίδοται	τίθεται	ἵσταται
διδόμεθα	τιθέμεθα	ἱστάμεθα
δίδοσθε	τιθέσθε	ἵστασθε
δίδονται	τίθενται	ἵστανται

[5] The form found in Lk.11:4 is ἀφίομεν.

§9   FORMS OF -IHMI

(1)   The only forms of the present middle and passive of -ἵημι found in the New Testament are

-ἵεται (3rd person singular)
-ἵενται (3rd person plural – Mk 2:5,9)

(2)   The present infinitive active of ἀφίημι is ἀφιέναι (Mk 2:7,10).

(3)   The imperfect of ἀφίημι is found as ἤφιον in the NT, as if it were not a compound verb.

> οὐκ ἤφιεν λαλεῖν τὰ δαιμόνια. (Mk 1:34)
> *He was not permitting the demons to speak.*

(4)   The imperatives of -ἵημι would be:

Present	-ίες	-ιέτω	-ίετε	-ιέτωσαν
Aorist	-ές	-έτω	-έτε	-έτωσαν

See Mk 7:27; Mt.6:12 for ἄφες used in two different senses.

(5)   Participles have forms -ιείς, -ιεῖσα, -ιέν (present); -είς, -εῖσα, -έν (aorist). They are declined like the aorist participle passive λυθείς, λυθεῖσα, λυθέν. The masculine and neuter follow the 3rd declension, having gentives in -ος (-ιεντος and -εντος) while the feminine follows the 1st declension, like δόξα – α impure.[6]

See Mk 8:13 – ἀφείς; Mk 1:18,20; 4:36; 7:8 – ἀφέντες.

[6] See 3§9(2).

§10   IMPERFECT INDICATIVE ACTIVE

Imperfect Indicative Active Tenses are:

ἐδίδουν	ἐτίθην	ἵστην
ἐδίδους	ἐτίθης	ἵστης
ἐδίδου	ἐτίθη	ἵστη
ἐδίδομεν	ἐτίθεμεν	ἵσταμεν
ἐδίδοτε	ἐτίθετε	ἵστατε
ἐδίδοσαν	ἐτίθεσαν	ἵστασαν
or ἐδίδουν	or ἐτίθουν	

See Mk 4:8; 6:7,41; 8:6 for ἐδίδου.
See Mk 3:6 for ἐδίδουν
See Mk 6:56 for ἐτίθεσαν.

§11   IMPERFECT INDICATIVE MIDDLE AND PASSIVE

Imperfect Indicative Middle and Passive Tenses are:

ἐδιδόμην	ἐτιθέμην	ἱστάμην
ἐδίδοσο	ἐτίθεσο	ἵστασο
ἐδίδοτο	ἐτίθετο	ἵστατο
ἐδιδόμεθα	ἐτιθέμεθα	ἱστάμεθα
ἐδίδοσθε	ἐτίθεσθε	ἵστασθε
ἐδίδοντο	ἐτίθεντο	ἵσταντο

§12   IMPERATIVES of ΔΙΔΩΜΙ

Notice the difference between the present imperative active of δίδωμι – δίδου, διδότω, δίδοτε, διδότωσαν – and the aorist – δός, δότω, δότε, δότωσαν. This affects the interpretation of the two forms of the Lord's Prayer. Mt.6:11 has the aorist imperative, suggesting that we need to pray every day for each day's supply of daily bread – "give us today (σήμερον) our daily bread", while Lk.11:3 has the present – "keep on giving to us every day (καθ' ἡμέραν[7]) our daily bread".

For another example of the aorist imperative, see Mk 6:37 – δότε.

[7] See 3§15(8).

§13 OTHER PARTS of ΔΙΔΩΜΙ in ΚΑΤΑ ΜΑΡΚΟΝ

(1) Most other parts of δίδωμι can be worked out from its principal parts and/or from the corresponding parts of λύω. Thus, δέδοται (Mk 4:11) is obviously 3rd person singular of the perfect indicative passive like λέλυται.[8]

(2) δοθήσεται (Mk 4:23) is derived from ἐδόθην (aorist passive[9]) but has the characteristic -θησ- of the future passive[10]; δοθῆναι (Mk 5:43) is similar to the aorist passive infinitive λυθῆναι[11]; δοθεῖσα (Mk 6:2) is also from ἐδόθην and is the feminine singular of the participle[12].

(3) δώσω (Mk 6:22,23) and δώσομεν (Mk 6:37) are both future active, while δοθήσεται (Mk 8:12) is future passive.

§14 AORIST of 'ΙΣΤΗΜΙ

(1) There are two forms of the aorist of ἵστημι – 1st aorist ἔστησα and 2nd aorist ἔστην. The 1st aorist is always transitive, i.e., it means *set, place, establish* something and so is usually followed by an object. The 2nd aorist, on the other hand (as well as the perfect and pluperfect active and all middle and passive forms[13]) is intransitive and means *stand*. The 2nd aorist participle is στάς, στᾶσα, στάν (see Mk 1:35).

(2) This is also the case in compound verbs; e.g., ἀνίστημι means *raise, appoint*; but the 2nd aorist ἀνέστη (Mk 3:26) is intransitive and means *rose up (against himself)*. Cf. ἐξέστη (Mk 3:21).

(3) σταθῆναι (Mk 3:24,25) is the aorist passive infinitive used intransitively and means *be established* or *stand*.

---

[8] See 6§7(4).
[9] See principal parts of δίδωμι in 11§4.
[10] See 6§9(1).
[11] See Appendix 1.
[12] See 7§4.
[13] See UBSD 88a.

(4) στήσητε (Mk 7:9) is 1st aorist subjunctive and therefore transitive. Its object is τήν παράδοσιν – . . . [so that] you may establish [your] tradition.

ASSIGNMENTS

PARSE

(1) παραδοθῆναι (Mk 1:14) [Cf. λυθῆναι – see 11§13(2)]

(2) παρέδωκεν (Mk 3:19) [See 11§6(1)]

(3) ἔδωκεν (Mk 2:26) [See 11§6(1)]

(4) ἐδίδουν (Mk 3:6) [See 11§10 – context will tell you person and number]

(5) ἐπέθηκεν (Mk 3:16,17) [See 11§6(1)]

(6) ἀναστάς (Mk 1:35) [See 11§14(1)]

(7) ἐξίστασθαι (Mk 2:12) [Cf. λύεσθαι – Appendix 1]

(8) ἀπεκατεστάθη (Mk 3:5) [Note double augment – cf. ἐλύθη]

(9) ἐξέστη (Mk 3:21) [See 11§14(2)]

(10) σταθῆναι (Mk 3:24,25) [See 11§14(3)]

(11) ἀνέστη (Mk 3:26) [See 11§14(2)]

(12) ἀφέντες (Mk 1:18) [See 11§9(5)]

(13) ἀφῆκεν (Mk 1:31) [See 11§6(1)]

(14) ἤφιεν (Mk 1:34) [See 11§9(3)]

(15) ἀφίενται (Mk 2:5) [See 11§9(1)]

(16) ἀφιέναι (Mk 2:7) [See 11§9(2)]

(17) ἀφεθήσεται (Mk 3:28) [From ἀφίημι – note -θησ-]

(18) ἀφεθῇ (Mk 4:12) [Note lengthening of ending – see 10§§1,2]

(19) ἀφίετε (Mk 7:12) [See 11§7]

(20) ἄφες (Mk 7:27) [See 11§9(4)]

(21) ἀφείς (Mk 8:13) [See 11§9(5)]

APPENDIX ONE

The Regular Greek Verb: First Conjugation

	Indicative	Imperative	Infinitive	Participle	Subjunctive	Optative
			ACTIVE			
Present	λύω	λῦε	λύειν	λύων	λύω	λύοιμι
Imperfect	ἔλυον	—	—	—	—	—
Future	λύσω	—	λύσειν	λύσων	—	λύσοιμι
Aorist	ἔλυσα	λῦσον	λῦσαι	λύσας	λύσω	λύσαιμι
Perfect	λέλυκα	λέλυκε	λελυκέναι	λελύκως	—	—
Pluperfect	(ἐ)λελύκειν	—	—	—	—	—

MIDDLE and PASSIVE

Present	λύομαι	λύου	λύεσθαι	λυόμενος	λύωμαι	λυοίμην
Imperfect	ἐλυόμην	—	—	—	—	—
Perfect	λέλυμαι	λέλυσο	λελύσθαι	λελυμένος	—	—
Pluperfect	(ἐ)λελύμην	—	—	—	—	—

MIDDLE

Future	λύσομαι	—	λύσεσθαι	λυσόμενος	—	—
Aorist	ἐλυσάμην	λῦσαι	λύσασθαι	λυσάμενος	λύσωμαι	λυσαίμην

PASSIVE

Future	λυθήσομαι	—	λυθήσεσθαι	λυθησόμενος	—	—
Aorist	ἐλύθην	λύθητι	λυθῆναι	λυθείς	λυθῶ	λυθείην

APPENDIX TWO

Principal Parts of Common Greek Verbs

Present	Future	Aorist	Perfect	Perf. M/P	Aorist Passive
λύω loose	λύσω	ἔλυσα	λέλυκα	λέλυμαι	ἐλύθην
ἀγγέλλω announce	ἀγγελῶ	ἤγγειλα	ἤγγελκα	ἤγγελμαι	ἠγγέλην
ἄγω lead	ἄξω	ἦξα / ἤγαγον	ἦχα	ἦγμαι	ἤχθην
ἀκούω hear	ἀκούσομαι	ἤκουσα	ἀκήκοα	—	ἠκούσθην
ἁμαρτάνω sin	ἁμαρτήσω	ἥμαρτον	ἡμάρτηκα	—	—
ἀποκτείνω kill	ἀποκτενῶ	ἀπέκτεινα	—	—	ἀπεκτάνθην
βαίνω go	βήσομαι	ἔβην	βέβηκα	—	—
βάλλω throw	βαλῶ	ἔβαλον	βέβληκα	βέβλημαι	ἐβλήθην
γίνομαι become	γενήσομαι	ἐγενόμην	γέγονα	γεγένημαι	ἐγενήθην
γινώσκω know	γνώσομαι	ἔγνων	ἔγνωκα	ἔγνωσμαι	ἐγνώσθην
γράφω write	γράψω	ἔγραψα	γέγραφα	γέγραμμαι	ἐγράφην
διδάσκω teach	διδάξω	ἐδίδαξα	—	—	ἐδιδάχθην
δίδωμι give	δώσω	ἔδωκα	δέδωκα	δέδομαι	ἐδόθην
ἔρχομαι come go	ἐλεύσομαι	ἦλθον	ἐλήλυθα	—	—

ἐσθίω eat	φάγομαι	ἔφαγον	—	—	—
ἔσθω (mainly in participle)					
εὑρίσκω find	εὑρήσω	εὗρον	εὕρηκα	—	εὑρέθην
καλέω call	καλέσω	ἐκάλεσα	κέκληκα	κέκλημαι	ἐκλήθην
κηρύσσω proclaim	κηρύξω	ἐκήρυξα	κεκήρυχα	κεκήρυγμαι	ἐκηρύχθην
λαμβάνω receive	λήμψομαι / λήψομαι	ἔλαβον	εἴληφα	εἴλημμαι	ἐλήμφθην / ἐλήφθην
λέγω say	λέξω / ἐρῶ	ἔλεξα / εἶπον	— / εἴρηκα	λέλεγμαι / εἴρημαι	ἐλέχθην / ἐρρέθην / ἐρρήθην
μανθάνω learn	μαθήσομαι	ἔμαθον	μεμάθηκα	—	—
ὁράω see	ὄψομαι	εἶδον	ἑώρακα / ἑόρακα	—	ὤφθην
πάσχω suffer	πείσομαι	ἔπαθον	πέπονθα	—	—
πείθω persuade	πείσω	ἔπεισα	πέποιθα	πέπεισμαι	ἐπείσθην
πέμπω send	πέμψω	ἔπεμψα	πέπομφα	πέπεμμαι	ἐπέμφθην
πίνω drink	πίομαι	ἔπιον	πέπωκα	—	ἐπόθην
πίπτω fall	πεσοῦμαι	ἔπεσον	πέπτωκα	—	—
στέλλω send	στελῶ	ἔστειλα	ἔσταλκα	ἔσταλμαι	ἐστάλην
τρέχω run	δραμοῦμαι	ἔδραμον	δεδράμηκα	δεδράμμαι	—
φέρω carry	οἴσω	ἤνεγκα / ἤνεγκον	ἐνήνοχα	ἐνήνεγμαι	ἠνέχθην
φεύγω flee	φεύξομαι	ἔφυγον	πέφευγα	—	—

REGULAR GREEK VERB: TABLES

INDICATIVE			
	Person	Singular	Plural
		ACTIVE	
Present	1st	λύω	λύομεν
	2nd	λύεις	λύετε
	3rd	λύει	λύουσι(ν)
Future	1st	λύσω	λύσομεν
	2nd	λύσεις	λύσετε
	3rd	λύσει	λύσουσι(ν)
Imperfect	1st	ἔλυον	ἐλύομεν
	2nd	ἔλυες	ἐλύετε
	3rd	ἔλυε(ν)	ἔλυον
Aorist	1st	ἔλυσα	ἐλύσαμεν
	2nd	ἔλυσας	ἐλύσατε
	3rd	ἔλυσε(ν)	ἔλυσαν
Perfect	1st	λέλυκα	λελύκαμεν
	2nd	λέλυκας	λελύκατε
	3rd	λέλυκε(ν)	λελύκασι(ν)
Plupft	1st	(ἐ)λελύκειν	(ἐ)λελύκειμεν
	2nd	(ἐ)λελύκεις	(ἐ)λελύκειτε
	3rd	(ἐ)λελύκει	(ἐ)λελύκεισαν

INDICATIVE			
	Person	Singular	Plural
		MIDDLE AND PASSIVE	
Present	1st 2nd 3rd	λύομαι λύῃ λύεται	λυόμεθα λύεσθε λύονται
Imperfect	1st 2nd 3rd	ἐλυόμην ἐλύου ἐλύετο	ἐλυόμεθα ἐλύεσθε ἐλύοντο
Perfect	1st 2nd 3rd	λέλυμαι λέλυσαι λέλυται	λελύμεθα λελύσθε λέλυνται
Plupft	1st 2nd 3rd	(ἐ)λελύμην (ἐ)λέλύσο (ἐ)λέλυτο	(ἐ)λελύμεθα (ἐ)λέλυσθε (ἐ)λέλυντο
		MIDDLE	
Future	1st 2nd 3rd	λύσομαι λύσῃ λύσεται	λυσόμεθα λύσεσθε λύσονται
Aorist	1st 2nd 3rd	ἐλυσάμην ἐλύσω ἐλύσατο	ἐλυσάμεθα ἐλύσασθε ἐλύσαντο
		PASSIVE	
Future	1st 2nd 3rd	λυθήσομαι λυθήσῃ λυθήσεται	λυθησόμεθα λυθήσεσθε λυθήσονται
Aorist	1st 2nd 3rd	ἐλύθην ἐλύθης ἐλύθη	ἐλύθημεν ἐλύθητε ἐλύθησαν

IMPERATIVE			
Present	Active	Middle/Passive	
Singular			
2nd	λῦε	λύου (from λυ-εσο)	
3rd	λυέτω	λυέσθω	
Plural			
2nd	λύετε	λύεσθε	
3rd	λυέτωσαν	λυέσθωσαν	
Aorist	Active	Middle	Passive
Singular			
2nd	λῦσον	λῦσαι	λύθητι
3rd	λύσατω	λυσάσθω	λυθήτω
Plural			
2nd	λύσατε	λύσασθε	λύθητε
3rd	λυσάτωσαν	λυσάσθωσαν	λυθήτωσαν
Perfect	Active	Middle/Passive	
Singular			
2nd	λέλυκε	λέλυσο	
3rd	λελυκέτω	λελύσθω	
Plural			
2nd	λελύκετε	λέλυσθε	
3rd	λελυκέτωσαν	λελύσθωσαν	

INFINITIVE		
	Active	Middle	Passive
Present	λύειν	λύεσθαι	λύεσθαι
Future	λύσειν	λύσεσθαι	λυθήσεσθαι
Aorist	λῦσαι	λύσασθαι	λυθῆναι
Perfect	λελυκέναι	λελύσθαι	λελύσθαι

PARTICIPLE

ACTIVE			
Present	**Masculine**	**Feminine**	**Neuter**
Singular			
Nom.	λύων	λύουσα	λῦον
Voc.	λύων	λύουσα	λῦον
Acc.	λύοντα	λύουσαν	λῦον
Gen.	λύοντος	λυούσης	λύοντος
Dat.	λύοντι	λυούσῃ	λύοντι
Plural			
Nom.	λύοντες	λύουσαι	λύοντα
Voc.	λύοντες	λύουσαι	λύοντα
Acc.	λύοντας	λυούσας	λύοντα
Gen.	λυόντων	λυουσῶν	λυόντων
Dat.	λύουσι(ν)	λυούσαις	λύουσι(ν)
Aorist	**Masculine**	**Feminine**	**Neuter**
Singular			
Nom.	λύσας	λύσασα	λῦσαν
Voc.	λύσας	λύσασα	λῦσαν
Acc.	λύσαντα	λύσασαν	λῦσαν
Gen.	λύσαντος	λυσάσης	λύσαντος
Dat.	λύσαντι	λυσάσῃ	λύσαντι
Plural			
Nom.	λύσαντες	λύσασαι	λύσαντα
Voc.	λύσαντες	λύσασαι	λύσαντα
Acc.	λύσαντας	λυσάσας	λύσαντα
Gen.	λυσάντων	λυσασῶν ·	λυσάντων
Dat.	λύσασι(ν)	λυσάσαις	λύσασι(ν)

Perfect	Masculine	Feminine	Neuter
Singular			
Nom.	λελυκώς	λελυκυῖα	λελυκός
Voc.	λελυκώς	λελυκυῖα	λελυκός
Acc.	λελυκότα	λελυκυῖαν	λελυκός
Gen.	λελυκότος	λελυκυῖας	λελυκότος
Dat.	λελυκότι	λελυκυίᾳ	λελυκότι
Plural			
Nom.	λελυκότες	λελυκυῖαι	λελυκότα
Voc.	λελυκότες	λελυκυῖαι	λελυκότα
Acc.	λελυκότας	λελυκυῖας	λελυκότα
Gen.	λελυκότων	λελυκυιῶν	λελυκότων
Dat.	λελυκόσι	λελυκυίαις	λελυκόσι

MIDDLE/PASSIVE			
Present	Masculine	Feminine	Neuter
Singular			
Nom.	λυόμενος	λυομένη	λυόμενον
Voc.	λυόμενε	λυομένη	λυόμενον
Acc.	λυόμενον	λυομένην	λυόμενον
Gen.	λυομένου	λυομένης	λυομένου
Dat.	λυομένῳ	λυομένῃ	λυομένῳ
Plural			
Nom.	λυόμενοι	λυόμεναι	λυόμενα
Voc.	λυόμενοι	λυόμεναι	λυόμενα
Acc.	λυομένους	λυομένας	λυόμενα
Gen.	λυομένων	λυομενῶν	λυομένων
Dat.	λυομένοις	λυομέναις	λυομένοις

Other middle and passive participles ending in -μενος, -μενη, -μενον are declined in a similar way, except that perfect participles middle and passive are always accented on the second last syllable: e.g., λελυμένος.

PASSIVE			
Aorist	Masculine	Feminine	Neuter
Singular			
Nom.	λυθείς	λυθεῖσα	λυθέν
Voc.	λυθείς	λυθεισα	λυθέν
Acc.	λυθέντα	λυθεῖσαν	λυθέν
Gen.	λυθέντος	λυθείσης	λυθέντος
Dat.	λυθέντι	λυθείσῃ	λυθέντι
Plural			
Nom.	λυθέντες	λυθεῖσαι	λυθέντα
Voc.	λυθέντες	λυθεῖσαι	λυθέντα
Acc.	λυθέντας	λυθεῖσας	λυθέντα
Gen.	λυθέντων	λυθεισῶν	λυθέντων
Dat.	λύθεῖσι(ν)	λυθείσαις	λυθεῖσι(ν)

SUBJUNCTIVE			
Present	Active λύω λύῃς λύῃ λύωμεν λύητε λύωσι(ν)	Middle/Passive λύωμαι λύῃ λύηται λυώμεθα λύησθε λύωνται	
Aorist	Active λύσω λύσῃς λύσῃ λύσωμεν λύσητε λύσωσι(ν)	Middle/Passive λύσωμαι λύσῃ λύσηται λυσώμεθα λύσησθε λύσωνται	Passive λυθῶ λυθῇς λυθῇ λυθῶμεν λυθῆτε λυθῶσι(ν)

OPTATIVE

Present	Active	Middle/Passive	
	λύοιμι	λυοίμην	
	λύοις	λύοιο	
	λύοι	λύοιτο	
	λύοιμεν	λυοίμεθα	
	λύοιτε	λύοισθε	
	λύοιεν	λύοιντο	
Future	Active		
	λύσοιμι		
	λύσοις		
	λύσοι		
	λύσοιμεν		
	λύσοιτε		
	λύσοιεν		
Aorist	Active	Middle	Passive
	λύσαιμι	λυσαίμην	λυθείην
	λύσαις	λύσαιο	λυθείης
	λύσαι	λύσαιτο	λυθείη
	λύσαιμεν	λυσαίμεθα	λυθείημεν
	λύσαιτε	λύσαισθε	λυθείητε
	λύσαιεν	λύσαιντο	λυθείησαν

Very few of these optative forms are actually found in the New Testament. See 2§5(8); 7§8; 7A6(21).

Subject Index

Biblical Index

(References in Assignments are not usually included here.)

Matthew					
1:19; 5:3	46	1:23	35, 45	3:22	34
6:9ff	7	1:25	19	3:24ff	48, 108
6:11f	106f	1:27	27n4, 35, 38	3:27	91n2
6:13	96	1:31	20, 35, 49, 105	4:3	86
6:24	90	1:32	87	4:5	13
7:17	49	1:33	35, 47	4:11	48, 108
9:18	98	1:34	104, 106	4:15	80, 94n10
10:29	27n4, 82	1:35	5, 108	4:17	87
12:23	82	1:38	96	4:21	82
14:21	56	1:39	47	4:23	35, 108
19:17	99	1:40	90, 99	4:27	35
19:20	67	1:41	35	4:30	97
22:11	13	1:44	96	4:31	51
24:34	97	1:45	35, 90	4:34	19f, 38, 40
26:41	81	2:1	19, 38	4:35	47
27:24	66f	2:2	92	4:36	27, 106
		2:5	104, 106	4:37	19, 27
Mark		2:6	86	4:38	13
1:1	30n5, 42, 68	2:7, 9	50, 104, 106	4:39	19, 78
1:2	12, 37, 42, 53	2:12	5, 40	5:2	88
1:3	23, 32, 37f, 42, 86	2:15	93	5:3	14, 91n2
1:4	37, 47, 86	2:17	93	5:5	35f, 60
1:5	49	2:19	53	5:9	35
1:6	34, 45, 86	2:20	37, 68	5:10	40
1:7	13, 40, 51, 53, 59	2:21	37, 51	5:11	35, 45
1:8	35, 45	2:23	36, 68, 93	5:14	35
1:9	37, 47	2:24	36, 55	5:22	34f
1:10	20, 35, 37	2:25	18	5:23	98
1:11	18, 46	2:26	36f, 55, 91	5:25	34f
1:12	19, 35, 38, 49	3:1	19, 35	5:26	51
1:13	20, 36	3:5	35, 87	5:29	35
1:14	79, 92	3:8	40	5:33–35, 40	34
1:16	19, 87	3:11	27n4, 60	5:43	108
1:17	18	3:13	35	6:2	108
1:20	18, 34, 106	3:14	97	6:9	67
1:21	19, 68f	3:16f	18, 35	6:10	98
		3:21	39, 108	6:11	34